HUMILITY

Matt Rawlins

Humility by Matt Rawlins.

Cover work by Kelvin Mark Tan at VERITAS. Thank you for being a friend and for your brilliant artwork.

Acknowledgment

I am grateful to John Feaver, Fiona Gifford and Pateenah Hordern for their thoughts and input into my writing. I also had the opportunity to work with a great new editor, Kay Ben-Avraham; she helped organize and clarify my thoughts that have been in different manuscripts sitting on my computer for ten years. Thank you.

OTHER BOOKS BY MATT RAWLINS

Rediscovering Reverence, the Path to Intimacy

Walking Naked into the Land of Uncertainty

The Question

The Namer

The Container

Mysteries Beyond the Gate &
other peculiar short stories

The Guardian

LEADERSHIP BOOKS FOR THE MARKETPLACE

BY MATT RAWLINS

The Green Bench
A dialogue about Leadership and Change

The Green Bench II
Ongoing dialogue about Leadership and Communication

Emails from Hell

The Lottery
A question can change a life

There's an Elephant in the Room
Discover the single most power tool for growth

Finding the Pain in your @ss-umption
A Leadership Tale

Courageous Relationships in Uncertain Times

Effective Leadership in Uncertain Times

Author's Note

Many years ago, I read Andrew Murray's book, *Humility: The Beauty of Holiness*. It came at a time when I was struggling under the burden of carrying a weight of wrong ideas about God and myself. The book started me on this journey and gave me a structure that helped me to find the path to freedom.

You will notice as you read that I have used some creative freedom in imagining the life of Moses. I am sure you will have your own perspective that will differ in places from mine. I am not trying to write about my perspective as the only truth to be understood, but to only try and understand him as a human struggling to find life. So where we may differ on his life, I ask for patience as I journey on this path to wholeness.

There's a passage in C. S. Lewis' *The Problem of Pain* in which he offers a story elaborating on the Biblical account of Creation. Before he launches into it, however, he explains the manner in which he offers this story: "What exactly happened when Man fell, we do not know; but if it is legitimate to guess, I offer the following picture—a 'myth' in the Socratic sense, a not unlikely tale." He goes on to define *myth* here as an account of what *may have been* historical fact.

I offer the stories in this book in the same light; the discussions and interactions I describe may be true, but only as they truly represent the ultimate truth of the ways of God and of our finite creation made in His image. As I imaginatively engage with the story of Moses, we look at his life through a filter: that of understanding humility. Scripture tells us that Moses walked in humility, and the fruit of it was that God called him a friend and spoke to him intimately.

Many of the interchanges and events are drawn directly from Scripture, but often I make leaps, conjectures, or expand the drama through imagination informed by the rest of God's revelation of himself in Scripture. As we study the Biblical account, it rarely gives us insight into what is going on inside of the characters. Often, the stories relate events without much of the psychology or inner struggles involved. It is almost as if God limits our view of these characters' internal world so that we may put ourselves in their places to try and understand them. As we all draw from the same well of humanity, perhaps in some sense, God makes it possible for us to understand anyone in the stories he tells us, simply through understanding God and ourselves.

And so I write from this two-fold grid: through the lens of God's character, and through the lens of human nature. For the first, I have studied hard to understand the nature and character of God. As a result, I have great confidence in Him: He is Big enough and Good to all. His story, given to us in His word, clearly displays His attributes. If I encounter something out of line with His character—my ultimate, clear guideline—then I immediately screen it out and wait for more understanding. My love for Him and for representing Him clearly gives me a focus to do this as authentically as I can.

The second part of the grid I use is my understanding of being human. All humans share a certain commonness, made in the image of God. In my years of working with others, and in my own soul-searching, I watch for those elements that we all share. If I dig deep enough, I can find the issues common to us all. Those heart issues I have tried to clarify in the stories told here.

Through the writing of this book, I have tried to be Biblical as well as humble myself. Where I have missed the mark and do not yet have the clarity or humility yet, I ask in advance for forgiveness, and I trust you will bear with me in my own limitations. This story, after all, is just one finite, broken man's view of a wonderful God: the true source of all humility.

—*Matt Rawlins*

TABLE OF CONTENTS

CHAPTER ONE

Introduction to Humility

He who sacrifices a whole offering shall
be rewarded for a whole offering;
he who offers a burnt-offering shall have
the reward of a burnt-offering;
but he who offers humility to God and man
shall be rewarded with a reward
as if he had offered all the sacrifices in the world.
—The Talmud

As I begin to write, I am struck by a statement hanging provocatively in my mind. Can I write it out? Do I even understand what it means after all these years? I will take the courage to put it on paper.

I am walking in humility.

The moment I've written it, I take a deep breath and want to back away from the screen. *Don't say that—that's pride!* I reflect. *Even if it could possibly be true, what would be the purpose of writing it?*

To put it simply, I want the grace of God in my life. I need it and desire it and am willing to take the risk to get it. It has not always been that way. It has been many years in the making. This book is my journey to understand humility, and to be at peace with God and who He made me to be.

When I step back from my initial gut reaction and let my mind respond, I realize I haven't done anything that hasn't already been modeled to us. The Apostle Paul, writing of his time in Asia, says, "You yourselves know, from the first day that I set foot in Asia, how I was with you the whole time, serving the Lord with all humility and with tears and with trials which came upon me through the plots of the Jews."[1] Is Paul being prideful? Or is there something else at work here?

Reading a journal article, I came across a comment by former president Bill Clinton; in an attempt to remove an unflattering portrait hung around his neck for three years, he urged Christian conservatives not to condemn "the motives and character" of people with whom they disagree, because if they "could look into my soul, they would see someone whose belief in God is as sincere and deep and genuine as theirs," and who probably is "much more humble in his Christian faith than many of them are."[2]

---

[1] Acts 20:18-19
[2] *U. S. News & World Report*, March 6, 1995.

By confessing my own humility, have I done what he did? How do I evaluate my statement? How do I evaluate his, or Paul's? I've struggled to understand humility for years, and in the past, if I called myself humble, I would have immediately thought I was walking in sin and needed to repent. Something in me would insist: *You can't say that yet because you still exist. True humility never knows it exists. You're not humble if you're aware of yourself being humble. And if you're claiming you're gifted in any area, that's pride.* Another part would say: *You make mistakes. If you were truly humble, you would never make mistakes.* Yet another part would seize up in terror, saying: *This is it. God finally has His chance to do all that painful stuff He loves to do to me. By claiming humility, I've basically given Him permission to hurt me in new ways.*

The confusion and fear make it tempting just to ignore the whole topic of humility entirely. And so many of us do, for most of our lives, like blindfolded archers trying to shoot at a target they refuse to aim for directly—loosing their arrows wildly and just hoping for the best.

Here's the problem: We are told to seek humility. "Seek the Lord,

All you humble of the earth who have carried out His ordinances; seek righteousness, seek humility. Perhaps you will be hidden in the day of the Lord's anger."[3] We can't hide from something, keeping it hidden or undiscussable, and at the same time still seek it and talk about it. A blindfolded archer has little chance of hitting the center of the target. Yet most of us do exactly that. In the back of our minds, we hope to just wake up one day and be humble. Unfortunately, it doesn't work that way. Humility is a choice, and if it is a choice, I must understand what I am choosing.

So here is our challenge: either we bring the struggle out in the open and face the terror of "losing" God's favor, or we leave the blindfold on and keep wasting our arrows, hoping we somehow stumble into grace, somehow hit the target.

Me? I choose to take the risk. If our loving God wants me to understand and pursue humility, it must be good for me. Let me say it again: Because God is righteous and gracious and calls me to walk with Him in humility, humility must be attainable and clear. I want that understanding.

I know you can hear me, God: *I ask You for humility*. I have asked before and continue to ask. You have given some—I want more.

Okay, I wrote it—much to the fear of my own flesh.

Want to join me in that prayer?

---

[3] Zephaniah 2:3

The road to humility can take a lifetime to travel. I am reminded of Paul's journey, recorded first to the Corinthians: "I am the least of the apostles."[4] Later in his life, he wrote to the Ephesians that he was "the very least of all saints."[5] Finally, near the end of his life, he wrote to Timothy that he was the foremost of sinners.[6] We are all on a journey: a growing revelation of who we are and who God is in us. I trust that as your understanding increases, the choice will become easier to make. You may be missing some wonderfully radical elements in your walk with God that just might set you free.

Picturing humility, I imagine swimming first in dirty water and then in clean. In the dirty water, I cannot see around me and quickly become lost. In clean water, everything is clear, and I have the right perspective on my surroundings. So it is with humility. The more humble I am, the more I can see life around me as it really is.

This brings us to our need of God. As we look at humility, we must first look to God. For in the end, humility is not as much about us as it is about God. It is about His life in us, permeating us, to help us live and understand the world around us.

---

[4] 1 Corinthians 15:9
[5] Ephesians 3:8
[6] 1 Timothy 1:15

The Most Humble Being in the Universe

Humility is one of the most misunderstood character attributes in the Bible. When God tells us, "Humble yourself," or "Seek humility," most of us would interpret this to mean that we have sinned and need to repent. In line with this, we assume that if we can detect no sin in ourselves, we are walking in humility. Although humility does deal with pride and includes repentance, its meaning goes far beyond these in richness and fullness. To see it, we must look to God—the most humble being in the universe.

There has never been, nor will there ever be, anyone more humble than God. He does not stand over us, looking down on us, in the image of an arrogant, power-hungry God. He serves us, and He calls us to join Him in His humility. Ultimately, humility is not for us—it is what *we* do for Him.

We can see this from two perspectives. From the first, He has to humble Himself simply to take notice of this tiny planet in its backwater solar system, hidden in a small galaxy of this vast universe. The Psalmist wrote, "The LORD is high above all nations; His glory is above the heavens. Who is like the LORD our God, who is enthroned on high, who humbles Himself to behold the things that are in heaven and in the earth?"[7]

---

[7] Psalm 113: 4-6

From the second perspective, He has shown His humility in coming to earth. He became a man and lived among us. He emptied Himself of His power and came as a man with no reputation, born in a manger, trained as a carpenter, raised in a small town, despised by society; He washed His disciples feet, grieved with others' pain, and died a humiliating death.

He is the most humble being in the universe, and He calls us to be like Him. Upon this and only this foundation can we go forward to seek and love humility.

When light passes through a prism, it splits into different spectrums or colors. A rainbow is the expression of light passing through the prism of water droplets in the air. As it is with light, so it is with humility. Three primary expressions of humility form the Biblical meaning of the word, and in this book, we will explore all three, for they form a complete whole. When we understand and practice each aspect, this comprehensive view of humility will open the door to the grace of God.

First, we are Created—we are finite. We don't know everything, and by our very nature, we are weak and limited. We can and will make mistakes and have to struggle and work hard to learn and grow. Either we can acknowledge with humility that we come from dust and to dust we will return, or we can spend our energies in a futile effort to control forces that will prove too much for us in the end.

Second, we are Sinners—We love darkness as a way to cloak ourselves from the pain of reality. In the face of our own conscious sins, we can humble ourselves before God and others, or we can choose pride instead of vulnerability, seeking to build up and protect our own image, and trying to destroy others' images in fits of jealousy.

Third, we are Saints—We each have a gift to offer, a unique voice used to express His glory. We are all called to be a part of His body, to express an aspect of His beauty. In humility, we can offer these gifts back to Him with gladness, or we can try to ignore, squelch, or neglect our gifts.

...

Imagine an artist focused on painting a small piece of canvas he has discovered. He starts to work without looking around at all, concentrating only on his desires for the piece, his own plans for how he wants his work to look. Now, imagine this artist standing back at last from his own labors. With each step backwards, he starts to see a bigger canvas: a grand painting on which someone else has been working for many years. His steps grow slower as he marvels at the intricacy and beauty of this unknown artist's masterpiece.

Suddenly, with a sinking of his stomach, he sees his own work: a dull, disconnected picture interrupting the harmony of the larger painting. He has been painting on someone else's masterpiece without a thought to the overall vision. Once he sees the bigger picture, what will he do? What choices will he make?

Humility as creation means asking ourselves these questions. In our finite, limited view, we didn't know about the larger canvas. As happens to all of us, when we do step back from our own narrow little lives and see the bigger picture—a masterpiece—what will we do about it?

> Will we, in anger, try to dismiss the masterpiece?
> Will we, in shame, try to deny our own work?
> Will we, in fear, feign ignorance, walk away, and hide?

This choice is ours, and we must learn to see it clearly. For though we face significant choices that are in our hands to decide, in many other areas of our lives, others' choices—not our own—created the canvas with which we have to work.

As it is today, so it was 3,500 years ago.

CHAPTER TWO

MOSES AND HUMILITY AS CREATION

Now the man Moses was very humble,
more than any man who was on the face of the earth.
Numbers 12:3

Miriam stood and stared at the basket. Her mother's voice interrupted her thoughts: "Put it in the river. Watch it closely as long as you can bear it."

Miriam still could not believe her ears. "Mom, we've hid him for three months. No one has found him. If you put him in the river, he'll die. Why can't we just keep him? Don't you love him?"

Miriam's mother gazed at the small figure of her son, sleeping in the woven basket. She finally replied, "I know this seems too painful to bear. I have wrestled with God, but there's nothing left we can do. If he stays with us, eventually they will hear him. If they hear him, they will kill him and us. You know they are killing all baby boys by order of the Pharaoh. What else can we do? I'm terrified he'll die, or maybe even worse, he'll be found by Egyptians, our oppressors for the last four hundred years. What if they find him and raise him to be one of them? That thought feels almost more painful than death itself. But I have to make a choice for him that he can't make for himself. Whether he lives or dies, he will be in God's hands."

Miriam took the child and walked slowly to the river. The weight of her mother's choice pressed down on her. The edict from Pharaoh weighed even heavier. Why should her brother die and she live, just because she was a girl and he was a boy?

Miriam put the basket in the shallow water watched her baby brother floating slowly downstream among the reeds. To her amazement and horror, a short while later, she watched the daughter of Pharaoh come out to the river at just the time little Moses began to float by. Pharaoh's daughter saw him, made a choice, and sent her servants to claim the crying baby as her own.

Moses would be a part of Pharaoh's household. Miriam's heart filled with fear. Yet in the midst of her terror, a crazy idea popped into her mind. She ran, came before Pharaoh's daughter, and asked if Miriam might bring a woman to help care for the child. Pharaoh's daughter gave her permission, and Miriam ran all the way home. Her mind could not rest. *My brother will be raised an Egyptian, but at least he will know his own mother,* she thought. She fought back her tears and dashed into their home to tell her mother what had happened.

...

Other people's choices affected Moses life. We are all born into a place and time with limitations, temptations, and struggles for those living in it. So it was for Moses; so it is for us. We are not just the end product of our own choices. Other people's choices deeply affect us as well. What others have chosen in the past can often influence us today. At a time and in a culture that breeds the illusion that we are self-made, we need a wake-up call.

As finite, limited creatures, we enter a race that has already been partly run:

- We did not choose to come into the world. Others made that choice, and no matter what their motives, the result is still the same: we had no say in our own birth.
- We did not choose the names given us at birth.
- We did not choose to bring sin into our world. It was already here when we arrived. We entered a world already darkened by others' choices.
- We did not choose to speak the language we speak, nor its influence on how we think.

- We did not choose to have the father, mother, brothers, or sisters we have—or didn't have.
- We did not choose our parents' vocation and economic status.
- We did not choose the weather or geography of our home.
- We did not choose our physical capacities or looks.
- We did not choose our personality.
- We did not choose where we went to school, or with whom.
- We did not choose what government ruled us, nor the decisions they made.
- We did not choose the technology, medical and otherwise, available to us.

But we do choose what we do with these influences. All of the choices made by those who have gone before us create a strong pull on us, a reservoir of influences. Moses was born into a life threatened by Pharaoh's choice to kill all Hebrew boys. His mother made a choice that put him in a river, and then Pharaoh's daughter made a choice that put him in Pharaoh's court. Because of their choices, Moses grew to become one of the most powerful men in Egypt.

There comes a time when someone passes us the baton: when our predecessors approach us and, in effect, say, "Now you choose what to do with your life."

But we have gotten ahead of ourselves. The story is still untold. Moses is still an infant in life with others making choices for him, and the days of learning humility are still ahead. How did Moses become the most humble man on the earth—so humble that God did not use dreams or hidden messages to speak with him, but instead spoke with him face-to-face?

...

We usually think humility means abasement. Surely, we think, the most humble man on earth would be born in a poverty-stricken family. His first memories of pain and suffering would provide the rich soil out of which humility could grow.

Not so for Moses. His first memories would have been of soft materials: being waited on hand and foot, with an abundance of every imaginable food. As he grew older, his will would have been supreme against all but Pharaoh, his Egyptian mother, and his brothers. The men and women around him would have striven to meet his every whim, knowing his happiness was their sole purpose in life.

From his earliest moments, most of his caregivers would train him to feel himself superior to everyone else. He could go anywhere, and no-one would dare stop his explorations. He could raise any question, and the wisest minds in the land would be available to answer it.

Any jokes he told would be laughed at. His friends would never make fun of him. No bullies would dare say a word against him. If he did get hurt, those who hurt him would quickly be made to apologize and to bow down before him. If he wished, he would never have to see them again.

Most of the people around him would have tried to convince him that he was a god—he did not make mistakes—he was special, unique, above all others. He would grow up believing he possessed more refined taste, greater strength, deeper wisdom, and broader capabilities than anyone else. If any of his subjects hinted he was in any way finite, on equal footing with the rest of humanity, it would probably cost their lives.

The world was his for the taking.

With our conception of humility, we might have written him off as hopeless, thinking that even God would find it impossible to produce humility out of such hard ground, such limitless privilege. But God's ways are different than ours. He is the most humble being in the universe, and true humility is not partial. He can teach humility in all circumstances.

Certainly Moses did not have a better start than us in achieving humility. If anything, Moses was at a disadvantage, as his early years would have made it much more difficult to become the most humble man on the face of the earth. The unfolding story of his life demonstrates just how much trouble he faced in turning from his background of comfort and privilege. His wake-up call, when it arrived, came loud and strong.

Humility as Creation

God is opposed to the proud, but gives grace to the humble.[8]

The root of *humble* and *human* is the same: *humas*, earth. We are dust. It is God who made us and not we ourselves. If you want to see your body's origin, rub your finger on a surface that hasn't been cleaned in a few days, and you will find the "stuff" of our bodies.

The first aspect of humility has to do with being created. We are finite, limited, weak, and vulnerable. In its simplest expression, it means that:

We will trip and fall.
We will make mistakes.
We will not know things.
We will not know what to do at times.
We will be unable to do certain things.
We will forget things we have learned.

---

[8] James 4:6

These mistakes are not sinful. They reveal limitation, not evil inclination. One of my favorite stories illustrating this is one I found in an Associated Press release:

Linda Burnett, 23, was visiting her in-laws, and while they went to a nearby supermarket to pick up some groceries, several people noticed her sitting in her car with the windows rolled up and with her eyes closed, with both hands behind the back of her head. One customer who had been at the store a while became concerned after an hour, and walked over to the car. He noticed that Linda's eyes were now open, and she looked very strange. He asked her if she was okay, and Linda replied that she'd been shot in the back of the head, and had been holding her brains in for over an hour. The man called the paramedics, who broke into the car because the doors were locked and Linda refused to remove her hands from her head. When they finally got in, they found that Linda had a wad of bread dough on the back of her head. A Pillsbury biscuit canister had exploded from the heat, making a loud noise that sounded like a gunshot, and the wad of dough hit her in the back of her head. When she reached back to find out what it was, she felt the dough and thought it was her brains. She initially passed out, but quickly recovered and tried to hold her brains in for over an hour until someone noticed and came to her aid.

You can see the painful logic of it; the assessment that the bread dough was her brain matter made sense. It was a great argument for a very awkward situation, but it was wrong. She made some assumptions, and they turned out to be just a little bit off. This is not sin. This is what it means to be human in a fallen world. We have to make some assumptions about life, and some of them will be wrong.

In the early 80s, my wife and I lived in Singapore and loved the city and the people there. We left in 1988 to move back to the States, and I would on occasion return to Singapore at different times to visit my friends and teach. On one of those trips, I arrived in the airport at midnight, and a close friend picked me up. I couldn't wait to eat some local food, so we stopped at a street restaurant, and I gleefully stuffed myself with as much *roti prata* and hot Indian curry as I could manage.

The next day, my friends wanted to go sailing, so we walked down to a friend's sailboat. At the harbor, I looked into the hold and noticed the messy bathroom; the owner said it was broken and getting fixed. I didn't think anything of it.

Slowly, the five of us moved out of the harbor into the open water between Singapore and Malaysia. There was not much wind, but we were enjoying being on the water with each other.

Then it hit. Not a tsunami—a nuclear war. In my stomach! I had eaten too much curry sauce last night, far too much for my out-of-practice stomach to digest. I could feel explosions going off in my bowels and wondered what to do. Holding it quickly became tortuous. I quietly caught the attention of my friend, who is also a medical doctor, and whispered to him of the disaster brewing inside me. He immediately asked the boat's owner to try and make land. As we inched along, I grimaced and tried to think of anything else but the war going on in my bowels.

It was no use. I finally sent the two girls to the front of the boat, took a bucket, went down into the hold, and relieved myself. I stuck my head back into open air, declaring, "There is death in this bucket." Seconds later, I had to go back down the stairs and tell the girls to keep away. After more "relief," I washed the nuclear waste over the side.

Not a terribly enjoyable experience. In fact, a humbling one.[9]

---

[9] Now for a painful confession. Just last month, in Singapore again on a visit, I hit the *roti prata* shop on my arrival. The next day, at a church speaking engagement, the apocalypse began again in my stomach. I got off the toilet, went to preach, and warned the people I might need to leave quickly. Thankfully I didn't. I then set up camp on the toilet until my next speaking engagement. Hopefully I am learning something here. (That I like *roti prata*? That I am a slow learner?)

Our bodies are weak, vulnerable, and can cause problems outside of our control, as anyone with a chronic or debilitating disease can attest. These problems are not always linked to sin. We simply have "dust" bodies, bodies with limitations in a fallen world. We can learn and grow in understanding of how our bodies react and thus limit their weaknesses somewhat, but we can never outgrow our bodies so that we are never susceptible or in need.

God describes us in Scripture in terms of weakness and limitations. Our lives quickly pass like shadows, breezes, or flowers in bloom: "For He Himself knows our frame; He is mindful that we are but dust. As for man, his days are like grass; as a flower of the field, so he flourishes. When the wind has passed over it, it is no more; and its place acknowledges it no longer." [10] Or again, "O Lord, what is man, that You take knowledge of him? Or the son of man, that You think of him? Man is like a mere breath; his days are like a passing shadow."[11]

To humble ourselves here—to grasp humility as Creation—is to embrace this weak and limited existence as a healthy and normal part of life, the way our Father created us. Rather than raging at weakness or vainly scheming and preparing ways to cheat the system and maintain control, we instead turn to God, like the Psalmist, and ask,

[10] Psalm 103:14-16
[11] Psalm 144:3-4

"Lord, make me to know my end
And what is the extent of my days;
Let me know how transient I am.
Behold, You have made my days as handbreadths,
And my lifetime as nothing in Your sight;
Surely every man at his best is a mere breath...
Surely every man walks about as a phantom;
Surely they make an uproar for nothing;
He amasses riches and does not know who will gather
them."[12]

I Don't Know

I used to hate those words. To admit that informa-
tion and life existed outside my knowledge was like
admitting defeat, throwing in the towel, or turning and
running with my tail between my legs. I love R. D.
Laing's poem describing this aspect of not knowing:

There is something I don't know
that I am supposed to know.
I don't know what it is I don't know,
and yet am supposed to know,
And I feel I look stupid
if I seem both not to know it
and not know what it is I don't know.
Therefore, I pretend I know it.
This is nerve-wracking

---

[12] Psalm 39:4-6

since I don't know what I must pretend to know.
Therefore I pretend to know everything.

I feel you know what I am supposed to know
but you can't tell me what it is
because you don't know that I don't know what it is.

You may know what I don't know, but not
that I don't know it,
and I can't tell you. So you will have to tell me everything.[13]

I wish I had a nickel for each time this happened—
each time someone asks me a question and I haven't
got the answer—each time people have that look on
their faces that tells me I should remember the event
they're talking about. I see the expectation in their
eyes; my stomach sinks, and before I know it, I nod as
though I recall it perfectly, when in actual fact, I don't
even remember the person's name. I used to want to
scream, *I don't know! I don't remember that place. I
have no memory of that. I don't remember you. I have
no idea how to make sense of all of this.* Yet instead, I
pretended knowledge and memory I didn't have.

One of the most freeing little revelations for me—*it
is okay not to know*—came during my graduate stud-

[13] R. D. Laing, *Knots* (New York: Pantheon Books, 1970), 56.

ies. I studied in my field for seven years. I knew it in-side and out. As I immersed myself in this narrow part of human knowledge, I realized how little people with a lot of education really know. They may know their field of expertise, but get a book or two outside of it and the playing field is leveled. So I started practicing a new sense of freedom: to ask the "stupid" question and admit I don't know. I still slip back to the pretense of knowledge from time to time, but slowly, I am moving in the opposite direction, toward humility. The more I practice it, the stronger it grows in me.

We can see in the Psalms that this simple admission of our limitations is actually the beginning of wisdom. We are called to number our days[14] and to be aware of our end[15] so that we may present to God a heart of wisdom. The beginning of wisdom is the simple ad-mission that we are weak, finite, and limited. Things bigger than me exist. I can't know it all. I can't do ev-erything. I can't remember everything. I can't walk and run without falling every once in a while. I came from dust and am returning to dust.

Up to this point, I have used light-hearted, even hu-morous, examples. Other more painful ones happen, in which we or others get hurt—again, not because of sin we commit, but simply because of our limited human-ity. Once, on a long flight, I stood in the aisle, trying

---

[14] Psalm 90:1-6
[15] Psalm 39:4-6

to get some relief from sitting for hours. A few others began to stand around me, so I decided to move on and lessen the congestion. I raised my arms to get them out of the way and turned around—*whack*—my arm connected with a hot dish of food the flight attendant was giving to another passenger. Suddenly the food was sent on its own flight! I'd meant no harm, but the food splattered everywhere, the passenger's specially prepared meal was gone, and the flight attendant, scrambling to clean up, glared at me where I stood. If looks could kill, I would not be here today. One look was all she needed to put me under. I writhed in awkwardness, apologizing, unable to set it right. This mistake, this exposure of my humanity, inconvenienced everyone around me.

What about when our limitation, despite good motives, causes almost unbearable pain? On the Oprah Winfrey Show one day, a woman shared her story. Driving home one day with her young son in his car seat, she stopped at 7-11 and ran in for a quick purchase. She absently left her keys in the car with her son still in the back seat. When she came out of the store, she saw someone jump in the car to steal it. Frantic, she ran around to her son's side, fumbling with the door. The car started to take off as she struggled to unbelt him—too late—she watched in horror as the car drove away and her son was dragged to death, stuck in the partially unlatched seat belt.

I hurt even writing this down. The potential pain connected to our good actions gone wrong is almost unbearable.

Life as finite creation happens on a spectrum. On the one side is humor—on the other side is unspeakable pain. But we must take a moment and remember the greatness of God. No matter what happens, He is greater than it. That is our only hope.

We are limited. Without God, this is a terror for us. If we don't know, who does? We are the brightest of the animal kingdom, the top of the list. If life is beyond us, then we are doomed to cause pain in others and ourselves, if for no other reason than that of our ignorance or inability. Life can hurt us immeasurably, even when we live it with good motives. The first step on the road to a wise response is humility—acknowledging our position as weak, limited, and needy—and turning to Him to care for us and reveal His thinking and heart to us.

Shame

When painfully confronted with our finite humanity, we face strong temptation to turn on ourselves, succumbing to caustic shame that can destroy us. I know the words well, the words that shout aloud in my mind, accusing me and shaming me for what I did. Whether it is knocking over hot food, forgetting passport details that cost someone else a trip, a car accident, or even a death, the words sound like this:

You should have known better.
You stupid fool, why didn't you…
I'm such a weakling…
    It's all my fault…
I'm the problem.
I never get it right.
I could have done it differently.
If I had only thought it through…

In the end, I conclude that I am flawed. I am tempted to think my limitation, my finitude (and therefore, my vulnerability) is the problem. Either I turn this against myself and wallow in self-loathing, or I become a control freak, aiming never to let anything get beyond my grip for fear of the damage I may cause.

This struggle is nothing new. In a sense, it was the very struggle in the Fall. You can see Satan's attempt to deceive Eve when he told her, "For God knows that in the day you eat from it, your eyes will be opened, and you will be like God, knowing good and evil."[16]

God had already made her in His image; that is, her character and capacity for choice already expressed what God had in mind. She could grow in it, but she

[16] Genesis 3:5

27

was already made in that image. Satan tempted her to be like God in a way that has caused more pain and suffering than she could possibly have imagined: to be powerful, strong, mighty, and experience the essence of life itself in her very nature.

This is a key point when understanding the difference between humility and shame, as they can seem very similar at a quick glance. Humility as Creation means that embracing our limitations is normal and healthy. When Satan came to Eve, he shifted her perspective to the assumption that normal life meant to be like God in our nature—that we should be powerful, knowing everything, never making mistakes, never running out of time, and able to do everything ourselves. When we can't manage that, we develop the underlying feeling that there is something fundamentally wrong with us. We feel not a conviction of sin, but rather a pervading shame, feeling that in essence, who we are is marred, spoiled, and wrong. Shame is the feeling that we are worthless because we are not like God in our nature and should be embarrassed about ourselves. We are finite, limited, created, and that makes us vulnerable.

Maybe you want to ask, *What was God thinking in making us this way?*

A better question is, "What are *we* thinking?" Our weakness was meant to be our joy, a glory, a celebration of the inferior before the Almighty. To discover you don't have to know it all, that you don't have to have it all together, that you can ask for help—this is one of the most basic and pure pleasures God meant for us to have. As C. S. Lewis describes it,

> I suddenly remembered that no one can enter heaven except as a child; and nothing is so obvious in a child—not in a conceited child, but in a good child—as its great and undisguised pleasure in being praised. Not only in a child, either, but even in a dog or a horse. Apparently what I had mistaken for humility had, all these years, prevented me from understanding what is in face the humblest, the most childlike, the most creaturely of pleasures—nay, the specific pleasure of the inferior: the pleasure of a beast before men, a child before its father, a pupil before his teacher, a creature before its Creator.[17]

This pleasure of being inferior, vulnerable, and weak before the Almighty God was offered to us as a blessing. However, we are so far from it that just writing it seems absurd. We see nothing pleasurable to us in humility. Just the sheer terror of being exposed and the potential pain we envision from that exposure is enough to turn our greatest heroes into wimps: they'll

---

[17] C. S. Lewis, *The Weight of Glory and Other Addresses*, revised ed. (New York: Collier Books, 1980), 12.

fight to the death to cling to ego and image, rather than facing vulnerability as an option.

Pascal wrote,

> I see only infinity on every side, hemming me in like an atom or like the shadow of a fleeting instant. All I know is that I must soon die, but what I know least about is this very death, which I cannot evade… When I consider the brief span of my life absorbed into the eternity which comes before and after—the small space I occupy and which I see swallowed up in the infinite immensity of spaces of which I know nothing and they know nothing of me, I take fright.[18]

It is a terrifying thing to see the unbelievable power around us and still embrace our limitations—even celebrate them.

Biblically speaking, Job provides one of the clearest examples of God's response to human limitation. The worst of the worst has happened to Job; he has lost everything: wealth, children, friends, health. The losses come faster than people can get the word to him. Yet in this adversity, he says, "Naked I came from my mother's womb, and naked I shall return there. The

---

[18] Blaise Pascal, *Penseés,* revised ed. (London: Penguin Classics, 1995), 130.

LORD gave and the LORD has taken away. Blessed be the name of the LORD."[19]

The simple admission of the created before the Creator: he acknowledges his place and who God is.

Job sits in the ashes, scraping the pus off his oozing sores. His friends come to visit him, saying he must have some secret sin for which God punishes him in this way. Job denies it. But the pain of being weak and vulnerable slowly eats away at him, and he wants to defend himself before God. How does God respond?

God shows up in a whirlwind and simply asks Job some questions.[20] Paraphrased, they sound like this:

> Now gather all your wisdom and I will ask you some questions, so you can instruct Me!
>
>> Where were you when I laid the foundations of the earth?
>> Who set its measurements? You do know this, don't you?
>> Who keeps the sea in place?
>> Have you ever in your life commanded the morning and caused the dawn to know its place?

---

[19] Job 1:21
[20] Job 38

God asks questions for four chapters about the world Job lives in, reminding Job of the characteristics of being God, and how far they outstrip the characteristics of being human. At last Job, seeing his weakness and limitations of knowledge, chooses humility and says, "I know that You can do all things, and that no purpose of Yours can be thwarted... Therefore I have declared that which I did not understand, things too wonderful for me, which I did not know... I have heard of You by the hearing of the ear; but now my eye sees You; therefore I retract, and I repent in dust and ashes."[21]

We see this same reaction in Simon Peter when Jesus gets into his boat and teaches the crowds from it. Jesus then tells Simon to put out his net, and Simon responds that they worked hard all night and caught nothing. But to please Jesus, Simon puts his net in and catches enough fish to almost sink two boats. "But when Simon Peter saw that, he fell down at Jesus' feet, saying, 'Go away from me, Lord, for I am a sinful man!' For amazement had seized him and all his companions because of the catch of fish which they had taken."[22] Confronted with his own limitations, he humbled himself.

Nebuchadnezzar came to the same point more reluctantly. A strong king over a vast kingdom, he had it all and considered it the work of his hands: "Is this not Babylon the great, which I myself have built as a royal

---

[21] Job 42:1-6
[22] Luke 5:8-9

residence by the might of my power and for the glory of my majesty?"[23] God then removed him from his position—and from his sanity. He ate grass like a beast of the field for seven years. At the end of that time, God returned his mind to him, and he humbled himself, declaring God's greatness and his own limitations.[24] He was just a man. God was God, and he was not.

Far better that we make that admission willingly, rather than being forced to it through humiliation. Jimmy Swaggart, a TV preacher years ago with a very large audience, was caught in sin. In his public confession, he said, "Maybe Jimmy Swaggart has tried to live his entire life as though he were not human…" He tried to act powerful, as though he were above humanity, ignoring that he too was weak and vulnerable. In the end, he had no grace from God to live this way, and his lack of humility destroyed him.

Even humiliation, like Swaggart's or Nebuchadnezzar's, can open the door to a relationship with God. Most of us don't discover God by clear argument of an objective truth, submitting to Him from rational conviction. Most of us dig a hole, get into trouble, and after floundering for as long as we can, at last admit we need help. The mess we've made proves we don't know as much as we wanted to pretend we did.

---

[23] Daniel 4:30
[24] Daniel 4:34-35

This lesson Paul learned the hard way. God gave him a "thorn in the flesh,"[25] and three different times Paul implored the Lord for it to leave him. God's word to Paul was, "My grace is sufficient for you, for power is perfected in weakness."[26] Translated, it means that God's power can only work perfectly through people who admit they are weak, human, or dust. Paul finally gets it: "Therefore I am well content with weaknesses, with insults, with distresses, with persecutions, with difficulties, for Christ's sake; for when I am weak, then I am strong."[27]

Paul had spent most of his Pharisaical life pursuing power, and God's desire was to give him grace for his weakness. We all may face various thorns in the flesh, as he did; we must learn that we cannot live outside of our human limitations, as he was trying to do. We will always be finite and limited. That is what it means to be human. When we are confronted with pain, when our assumptions that we should be powerful, knowing, and all-capable are exposed, God extends us an invitation to remind us, as finite creation, of our desperate need for an infinite God. He offers an opportunity to walk with Him through it.

I remember watching my mother die of cancer, feeling the small tumors bulging out from her skin. The gift

---

[25] 2 Corinthians 12:7
[26] 2 Corinthians 12:9
[27] 2 Corinthians 12:10

of love in weakness we shared in that time of pain, just walking down the road to death, is a precious memory for me.

The first time I glimpsed my son, born premature and weighing 3.3 pounds, he looked like a little refugee. I could put my thumb and forefinger all the way around his chest in a circle. The doctor told me that they didn't know how much oxygen to give a premature baby: too much, and they ruin his eyes; not enough, and they can cause brain damage. I listened, utterly helpless—so deeply painful and humbling. My wife and I quickly turned to God and asked for His grace to walk with us through this painful time.

And then I watched my older brother die of bone cancer. The day he died, I went to get his kids at school. I brought the two older ones home, and I watched Micah crawl up on his dead father's lap and cry himself to sleep. The agony of it tore my heart open anew.

Learning to embrace the pain of weakness, an inability to fix anything, solve anything, or stop anything, brings us face to face with the constant truth of our need for God. We don't need Him more at certain times than at others. My awareness of my need for Him changes on a moment-by-moment basis, but it does not affect the reality of how much I need Him. My mother, brother, and son all needed God just as much when they were healthy as when they were sick. I need Him now, even when I don't feel like it. God holds our very being together by His power. We are absolutely, universally dependent on God: His power, His wisdom, His presence holding reality together. He did not create a world and then leave it alone; He must sustain it, in each moment, continuously.

To be honest, I don't know how those without faith in a caring God do it. They know deep down that they are vulnerable, but they cannot relax into weakness and humility; they must always be on guard. They have to figure it all out—in a sense, be god—a role not designed for us and therefore exhausting, impossible. As Christians, we don't have to know all the answers or even be in control, because we know someone who does know, someone Big enough to deal with them. I think this is what it means to be childlike in our faith. We may not know the answers, but we know that our Father knows, and He will make it right. That is enough for us.

In many ways, this question of how to handle our inevitable human weakness forms a major difference between the kingdoms of this world and the Kingdom of God.

The kingdom of this world venerates strength and power. It sees being limited and vulnerable as a sign of weakness, to be avoided at any cost. The Kingdom of God, however, sees that everything is weak and vulnerable before the power of its Creator. We may celebrate weakness as an opportunity for God to touch us through His power.

But we can't stop here. Embracing weakness is the starting point for finding the grace of God. Remember, abundant life is offered to us, and we must not stop until we have it. We have already looked at embracing our creaturely limitations. Now we must ask: what about sin? What do we do with the choices we have made?

CHAPTER THREE

HUMILITY AS A SINNER

From the start, we must clearly differentiate between *humility as creation* and *humility as a sinner*: the humbling of pride. While interdependent, the two are very different. The first kind of humility usually invades our lives without giving us much choice in the matter; we don't purposely choose to fall down, we don't choose to make stupid mistakes, and we don't choose to lose control of the forces around us; it's simply a part of life in our world. Our only choice concerns what we do with this new knowledge we have about our limitations.

Humility as a sinner, a choice rooted in pride, goes beyond simple limitations. Years ago, I watched an unmarried late night talk show host sharing with a guest that often, when he (the host) is in bed with a woman, he talks to God and senses his need for Him. He recognized his creaturely limitations and weakness, but he never progressed beyond that basic humble acknowledgment, instead living a life of arrogance and self-gratification through his moral choices. One aspect of humility is not enough.

Pride—the root of what defines us as "sinners"—is yet the hardest thing to see in our own lives. The more you have of it, the harder it is to see: just as the more asleep you are, the less you know of waking. Only the awake person can truly understand sleep. You can only truly understand pride when you have humbled yourself, but proud men and women will not want to make the attempt. The proud man knows nothing of pride because it has blinded him. We must get the very thing we don't have—humility—in order to get the very thing we most sorely need—relationship—but pride keeps us from seeing our need.

Pride is the hardest thing for us to see because it affects every area of our lives. We are nurtured with it as a child, force-fed it with peer pressure in school, and then pushed out into a world saturated with it. Eventually we begin to suspect something is wrong, but as with a wife who stays with an abusive husband, the known pain is better than the unknown. So instead of trying to find something better, we keep our pride, believing the known pain it causes us (and others) is better than the unknown pain of humility.

Defining pride, however, can be an almost impossible task. It's a bit like trying to fix your glasses. You take them off to see what's wrong, but then you can't see anything without your glasses. What we can do, however, is start by looking for the fruit of pride in our lives. If the fruit is there, the root of pride will be there as well.

Fruit of Pride

The Bible defines success not as wealth, genius, or importance, but as intimacy. You are successful in the eyes of God not by making a lot of money, nor by having incredible, stand-out intelligence, nor by being famous. No, you are successful in the eyes of God if you walk in intimacy with Him and others. It's that simple—and yet, it is the hardest work we could do.[28] We could frame pride in a variety of different ways, but I frame it here in its most insidious manner: in light of how it destroys our ability to be successful (i.e. relate well to God and each other).

Nowhere does this show more painfully than in Adam and Eve. When they lived free of pride, Scripture tells us, "And the man and his wife were both naked and were not ashamed."[29] However, as soon as they chose pride, they felt shame, covered their nakedness (vulnerability), and hid from God.

As with them, so with us: pride destroys our ability to relate and thus be successful. It destroys who we were made to be. In the end, we become like Adam and Eve, covering ourselves and hiding from God and others. Let us examine how this occurs.

---

[28] I speak here not of physical or sexual intimacy, but rather the ability to be vulnerable, open, and authentic in relating to God and others.

[29] Genesis 2:25

We lust for power. The single most destructive element in any relationship is the abuse of power. To the degree a relationship is built on power, to that degree is love—and thus, life—missing from it.

Satan offered to the woman the lie that if she ate of the forbidden fruit, she would be like God, knowing good and evil.[30] The key, of course, is she was already like God. Adam and Eve were made in His image, the Bible says. This had to do with their character and their capacity to choose. In essence, they were capable of self-direction and had responsibility for their choices. They were to be like Him in His righteousness, justice, love, mercy, grace, and humility. They could choose His ways and grow ever more beautiful as their lives expressed His character. So what was Satan talking about?

As we examined earlier, the lie was that they would be like God in their nature—having the power to experience things no other part of creation could experience. We are by nature limited and finite. God made us with a healthy and natural desire to grow more and more like Him. Yet Satan's clear, bold lie twisted our natural desire from *growing* (as God intended) to *seizing*: not being content to be finite and grow at God's pace, but instead looking for a shortcut, to take the process into our own hands, and to be like God in His nature. This opened the door for turning our natural de-

---

[30] Genesis 3:5

sire for power into a lust for power, all-consuming in our arrogant lives.

C. S. Lewis said it this way:

> What Satan put into the heads of our remote ancestors was the idea that they could "be like gods"—could set up on their own as if they had created themselves—be their own master—invent some sort of happiness for themselves outside God, apart from God. And out of that hopeless attempt has come nearly all that we call human history—money, poverty, ambition, war, prostitution, classes, empires, slavery—the long terrible story of man trying to find something other than God which will make him happy.[31]

German philosopher Friedrich Nietzsche argued that this hunger (for power) is the essence of our humanity. The "will to power," he said, is the basic human drive—more basic than all other human needs. Since the beginning, we have always fought, or chosen to feed, this perverted craving to control one's destiny, to be free to realize one's full potential without restraints from anyone—including God.

As can be seen here, power provides simply the means to the ultimate goal: control. The purpose of

---

[31] C. S. Lewis, *Mere Christianity* (New York: MacMillan Publishing Co., 1960), 53.

control is *pleasure* (getting what I want, when I want it) and *safety* (never getting hurt). The use of power in relationships, then, is the capacity one has to determine what happens: the capacity to make others yield to my wishes, even against their will. By definition, no relationship built on power can survive, because power and control negate relationship. If I control my loved one, I make my loved one merely an extension of myself. No relationship exists between me and myself. When I bring power into relationship, making others objects to be used for my own pleasure and self-gratification, I erase relationship entirely.

But for many of us, the fear of rejection is so painful that the very whiff of it in a relationship will send us running to get control as quickly as possible. We use many avenues to secure power for ourselves: possessions, knowledge, position, you name it. Robert Greene wrote a popular book called *The 48 Laws of Power*, [32] an interesting read that describes the very essence of life here in our fallen world. Some of these laws illustrate perfectly the sickness of the lust for power, and how its methods are diametrically opposed to the ways of God, the ways that make for success, life, and love. (In places, I will include comments in parentheses to clarify the heart of what I think he's saying.)

---

[32] Robert Greene, *The 48 Laws of Power* (New York: Viking Press, 1998).

- Law 1: Never outshine the master. (Respect the power brokers so you can get what you want.)
- Law 2: Never put too much trust in friends, and learn how to use enemies… You have more to fear from friends than from enemies.
- Law 3: Conceal your intentions—Keep people off balance and in the dark by never revealing the purpose behind your actions.
- Law 5: So much depends on reputation— Guard it with your life. (Self-exaltation is all that matters.)
- Law 6: Court attention at all costs.
- Law 7: Get others to do the work for you, but always take the credit.
- Law 8: Make other people come to you—Use bait if necessary. (Set traps to capture people and then use it against them.)
- Law 11: Learn to keep other people dependent on you. (In order to be in control, you must always make sure others need and want you.)
- Law 12: Use selective honesty and generosity to disarm your victim. (Truth is irrelevant.)
- Law 14: Pose as a friend, work as a spy. (Knowledge is power: get it and use it.)
- Law 17: Keep others in suspended terror: Cultivate an air of unpredictability. (Do not expose yourself and let others know you. Keep them insecure so you can be secure.)

- Law 20: Do not commit to anyone—Play people against one another. You cannot allow yourself to feel obligated to anyone—To commit yourself to anybody or anything is to be a slave.
- Law 21: Play a sucker to catch a sucker—Seem dumber than your mark. If they think they are smarter, they will never suspect you are having ulterior motives.
- Law 27: Play on people's need to believe to create a cult-like following. (Manipulate people's desire for faith in something bigger than themselves.)
- Law 31: Control the options: Get others to play with the cards you deal. The best deceptions are the ones that seem to give the other person a choice. Your victims feel they are in control, but they are actually your puppets.
- Law 33: Discover each man's thumbscrew. (Use others' pain for your advantage.)
- Law 36: Disdain things you cannot have: Ignoring them is the best revenge. The less interest you reveal, the more superior you seem.
- Law 38: Think as you like, but behave like others. (You must be accepted by others in order to control them.)
- Law 39: Stir up waters to catch fish—Find the chink in their vanity through which you can rattle them, and you hold the strings.

- Law 40: Despise the free lunch. (Anything free is dangerous: watch out, it will cost you something in the long run.)
- Law 42: Strike the shepherd and the sheep will scatter. Trouble can be traced to a single strong individual. Neutralize their influence by isolating or banishing them.

Green summarizes,

> The most important of these skills, and power's crucial foundation, is the ability to master your emotions. An emotional response to a situation is the single greatest barrier to power, a mistake that will cost you a lot more than any temporary satisfaction you might gain by expressing your feelings. Emotions cloud reason, and if you cannot see the situation clearly, you cannot prepare for and respond to it with any degree of control... You cannot succeed at deception unless you take a somewhat distanced approach to yourself—unless you can be many different people, wearing the mask that the day and the moment require... Playing with appearances and mastering arts of deception are among the aesthetic pleasures of life. [33]

---

[33] Greene, *48 Laws.*

"In fact," Greene writes, "the better you are at dealing with power, the better friend, lover, husband, wife, and person you become."

Really? Look at the power-hungry human race, most of whom have been practicing these sorts of tactics all our lives. How successful is humanity? Are we all happy in our relationships? Do we die in peace with those we love around us, feeling no regrets?

Now, take a deep breath and realize—that is the polluted air we have been breathing our whole life. It is the very life of the flesh. Given an inch, it will take a mile. Or, better said, given any room in any relationship, it will destroy it like a raging cancer.

In the kingdom of God, when I use power in a relationship to get others to do something they don't want to do, I am moving in pride.[34] Love and power stand in opposition to each other; you cannot express love and power at the same time.

Erich Fromm said, "The lust for power is not rooted

---

[34] Exceptions exist here, most notably in the parenting relationship. Sometimes a father will make a child do something the child doesn't want to do (eat vegetables, for example), but he does it for the child's good, not in order to meet the father's own needs or desires. Pride cares about what *I* want, whereas in humility, I care about getting to what *God* wants, whether for myself or others. Regardless, even in parenting, making a child obey against his or her will is a last resort in any situation.

in strength but in weakness."[35] The paradox is that the weaker we feel, the more we crave power for our own protection. So if we humble ourselves as creation and embrace our limitations, we must take care to also humble ourselves with regards to our pride. Otherwise, we will seek out the world's power to protect us and miss out on the very purpose of our weakness: to enhance our dependence on our relationship with God.

How do I know I cling to power and control in a relationship?

- I am unwilling to have my opinions opposed or corrected.
- I am insensitive to the feelings of others.
- I am more concerned with what I get out of the relationship than what I can give.
- I maintain the relationship by force, whether through physical, emotional, spiritual, or psychological domination.
- I am not accountable to others for my choices; I am a law unto myself.
- I do not expose my own weaknesses or feelings.
- I keep my agenda hidden and use only the facts that benefit my desires.

---

[35] Eric Fromm, *The Art of Loving* (New York: Harper Perennial, 2006).

All other abuses of pride will grow out of this one area, and therefore, the strongest root must be dealt with most severely. To humble ourselves in regards to power means fundamentally changing the way we approach relationships. And the first step in that work is asking forgiveness where we have used power to violate relationships.

We are competitive. Another marker of pride's hold in our lives is in our competitiveness. I have seen the pain of this in my own family. My dad was the youngest of nine boys and one girl. Grandpa and Grandma came out from the dust bowl days in Oklahoma in an old Model T and headed west with everything they owned in the car. Their struggle to survive brought about an environment of competition among the boys. Dad got caught up in it and had to prove he was somebody through sports and education. He got his PhD from UCLA and set out to prove to the brothers—and the world—that he was Somebody. I remember as a young child hearing the brothers talk about sports and who could do what. Softball, football, golf, running: you name it, and they competed to prove themselves strongest or best.

I have had ongoing and growing revelation of this in my own life. The last few months brought new awareness of how insidious and destructive this aspect of pride can be. Struggling with my relationship with God and not sure why, I talked it through with a friend, who helped me recognize that I related to God as I would relate to my family: competing, proving, achieving. I'd been believing many things: *I must accomplish something, or God will not use me. What I do defines me. God doesn't really want what is best for me; He just wants to use me to accomplish something He needs done.*

It shocked me, how deeply this had taken root in my heart. But I saw it, and then I knew why I was struggling. I was living with a bent concept of God, and I needed help to straighten it out.

Challenge and competition are very different. Challenge is built on different gifts and abilities in people provoking us to give more or do better; it involves no sense of "winner take all." Competition says that my relationships are defined by winning. When I win, I will have good relationships. That is a blatant lie. What happens in reality when two competitive people try to relate? In essence, true relationship becomes impossible. As C. S. Lewis writes:

> Each person's pride is in competition with everyone else's pride... Two of a trade never agree... Pride is essentially competitive—by its very nature—while other vices are competitive only, so to speak, by accident. Pride gets no pleasure out of having something, only out of having more of it than the next man. We say that people are proud

of being rich, or clever, or good-looking, but they are not. They are proud of being richer, or cleverer, or better-looking than others. If every one else became equally rich, or clever, or good-looking, there would be nothing to be proud about. It is the comparison that makes you proud: the pleasure of being above the rest... Power is what pride really enjoys: there is nothing makes a man feel so superior to others as being able to move them about like toy soldiers. If I am a proud man, then, as long as there is one man in the whole world more powerful, or richer, or cleverer than I, he is my rival and my enemy... In God you come up against something which is in every respect immeasurably superior to yourself. Unless you know God as that—and, therefore, know yourself as nothing in comparison—you do not know God at all. As long as you are proud you cannot know God... A proud man is always looking down on things and people: and, of course, as long as you are looking down, you cannot see something that is above you... [36]

We are unbroken. Of course, we are already broken from the choices we have made. Sin has broken us; that's a reality. But do we admit it? When we sin, do we ignore and deny it, or do we own up to what we've done? Do we admit we need forgiveness just as much

---

[36] C. S. Lewis, *Mere Christianity*.

as those around us? Or will we listen to our deceitful heart, which wants to hide any brokenness?

For the last eight years, I've taken a Korean version of martial arts with a local pastor. Sparring (practice fighting) with our gear on one night, my 17-year-old (skinny) opponent took what I felt was a cheap shot at me. Immediately, my anger flared. *You want to fight?* I thought. *Bring it on.* I gave him something to think about. It only took a few minutes, and it felt good, getting to vent my anger. Only afterward did I question whether my response was appropriate.

After I settled down, I apologized for getting so aggressive. But within a couple of weeks, this young man quit the class. *Lord,* I realized, *I am still unbroken.* When someone pushes me, I'm threatened by it. I have to show I can deal with it. I needed to prove I could keep up with a younger kid. So I chose my pride—and that young man paid the price.

A broken man is a servant of one with greater power. A broken man does not hold his personal desire as supreme. He doesn't have to defend himself to prove anything. A broken man does not fear brokenness: he has already faced that pain and knows it cannot harm him. He allows others to see it, because in the brokenness, he finds the riches of God at work.

Paul Billheimer described brokenness in this way:

One is not broken until all resentment and rebellion against God and man is removed. One who resents, takes offense, or retaliates against criticism and opposition or lack of self-appreciation is unbroken. All self-justification and self-defense betrays an unbroken spirit. All discontent and irritation with providential circumstances and situations reveals unbrokenness. Genuine brokenness usually requires years of crushing, heartache, and sorrow. Thus our self-will surrendered and deep degrees of yieldedness and submission develop, without which there is little *agape* love.[37]

We live in the fear of Man. This is one of the most subtle and deceiving aspects of pride. *Fear* in this sense refers not to a frightened animal but rather refers to reverence, awe, respect, or honor. Who is your audience? The simple truth is that the ones whose attention and applause we want most will be the ones we want to please the most. If we value people's attention more than God's, we can be assured that the fear of man is defining and guiding us.

I grew up in a Christian home wanting to be a good boy, to do what was right. I tried hard to please people. Because I didn't do anything *really* bad to others, I thought I was a good kid.

---

[37] Paul Billheimer, *Destined for the Throne: How Spiritual Warfare Prepares the Bride of Christ for Her Eternal Destiny* (Minneapolis, MN: Bethany House Publishers, 2005).

I never understood what was truly happening beneath the surface: the degree to which pride and the fear of man was destroying me. I wasn't honest about what was really going on inside of me. I wasn't real with others. I just stuffed it all and tried to please everyone. I didn't accept any weakness from myself; I would compete to win to please my dad. I would wear socially acceptable clothes to fit in. I did whatever I needed to do to be safe. But I was consumed with the fear of man: if people liked me, I figured I was OK. If they didn't, then I wasn't.

King Saul operated on a similar line. God, through the prophet Samuel, told Saul clearly to go and destroy the Amalekites—a people who used to sneak up on Israel and cut open their pregnant women. God had had enough of this people's sin. Saul was to be God's instrument to judge them. He was to completely destroy them. Instead, Saul kept the best animals alive and didn't kill their king. When Samuel confronted him, he replied,

> "I have sinned; I have indeed transgressed the command of the LORD and your words, because I feared the people and listened to their voice. Now therefore, please pardon my sin and return with me, that I may worship the LORD."

> But Samuel said to Saul, "I will not return with you; for you have rejected the word of the LORD,

and the LORD has rejected you from being king over Israel."

And as Samuel turned to go, Saul seized the edge of his robe, and it tore. So Samuel said to him, "The LORD has torn the kingdom of Israel from you today, and has given it to your neighbor who is better than you. And also the Glory of Israel will not lie or change His mind; for He is not a man that He should change His mind."

Then [Saul] said, "I have sinned; but please honor me now before the elders of my people and before Israel, and go back with me, that I may worship the LORD your God."[38]

Even as Saul admitted his sin, he still cared most about being seen and honored before the people—not about repenting and beginning to right his wrongs. God declared He would take the kingdom from Saul, but he still cared for nothing else but being honored before the people. He was more in awe of them and their opinion of him than of God.

God asks Israel,

Who are you that you are afraid of man who dies,
And of the son of man who is made like grass;
That you have forgotten the LORD your Maker,

---

[38] 1 Samuel 15:24-30

Who stretched out the heavens,
And laid the foundations of the earth…?[39]

They had lost their reverence for God and became consumed with what the people around them thought. We struggle with this in each generation. Jesus confronted it among the religious leaders of his day:

You are those who justify yourselves in the sight of men, but God knows your hearts; for that which is highly esteemed among men is detestable in the sight of God.[40]

And when you pray, you are not to be as the hypocrites; for they love to stand and pray in the synagogues and on the street corners, in order to be seen by men. Truly I say to you, they have their reward in full.[41]

But they do all their deeds to be noticed by men; for they broaden their phylacteries, and lengthen the tassels of their garments.[42]

Woe to you, scribes and Pharisees, hypocrites! For you are like whitewashed tombs which on the outside appear beautiful, but inside they are full of dead men's bones and all uncleanness.[43]

---

[39] Isaiah 51:12-13
[40] Luke 16:15
[41] Matthew 6:5
[42] Matthew 23:5
[43] Matthew 23:27

We refuse the truth and choose blindness. Scott Peck uses the words "militant ignorance" to describe our problem.[44] I love those words; they fit so well. The problem is not that we don't know the truth—it's that we don't *want* to know the truth. We keep a vigilant watch to make sure we don't learn anything that makes us feel bad, look bad, or brings on any level of guilt.

Pride wants to maintain control over what is true or real. Giving that control away to someone else makes us vulnerable. Pride therefore uses the tool of unbelief—willful, militant ignorance—to protect itself, declaring in essence, "I will say what is true and real, and anything I don't want to be real, won't be."

The more you refuse to obey what you know is right, the more unbelief will grow, because you need it to justify the life you have lived. The Bible says the pride of our heart deceives us.[45] This militant ignorance destroys our relationships because it keeps us out of the light. Instead of letting that light shine on all parts of us, the good and the bad, we only hear and deal with things as we want them to be. We refuse to see, hear, or admit anything that does not fit into our image of reality—and ourselves.

---

[44] M. Scott Peck, *People of the Lie: The Hope for Healing Human Evil* (New York: Touchstone, 1998).

[45] Jeremiah 49:16; Obadiah 1:3

We only exert authority; we do not submit to it.
There are two conditions for wielding authority. First,
you must be wise enough or big enough to know what
to do; but second, you must have the character to do it
even at your own expense.

Pride rejects anyone else's authority and insists on
always being the one to wield it. Unfortunately, someone who can't be under authority is the last person who
can be trusted to handle authority correctly. But pride
hates that anyone would have authority to tell it what to
do, and therefore, prideful people will always struggle
with anyone in authority over them. Pride hates the
thought that somebody else could determine what is
best for them. After all, their self-exalted view of themselves tells them they know best.

Now, the key to figuring out rightful authority has
to do with defining who we are. If we are all there is,
then we can claim authority. We can live for the here
and now and forget anything else. If, however, someone else made us and knows far more about the running
of the world (remember God's reply to Job?) and our
lives' beginning and end, then ultimate authority belongs to Him. Arrogance says my pleasure and safety
right now is the most important thing in life. Humility
says short-term pleasure and safety—at the cost of reality, relationships, and authenticity—is not worth it; it
relinquishes the pursuit of pleasure and instead trusts
God. God is the only one wise enough or big enough to

know what must be done, and He is the only one good enough to do it for the benefit of all concerned.

We focus on self-exaltation. Most people know about this aspect of pride; in fact, most people think that pride and self-exaltation are the same thing, when in reality, self-exaltation is only one of pride's many symptoms. Self-exaltation implies that we can choose how to create greater value for our own life: how to increase our importance and earn more respect, worth, and love.

Because of the effects of the fall and sin in our world, we all struggle with our value. When we're honest, we know we have done things wrong and are in trouble. We know we shouldn't be loved or valued, and in pride we want to prove we can make up for it and earn back the love and value we know we so desperately need.

In my life, I tried to do that earning through education. I went to college for a couple of years and learned how to act stupid. God took hold of my heart, and I went into missions overseas for almost ten years in Asia and the Pacific. I came home and went back to school with a changed heart, graduating ten years later with a PhD. I did the degree work for God—but even so, after I finished, something sinister started to happen. In all types of conversations with others, I would find creative, convoluted ways to tell people that I had my PhD. *Why am I doing this?* I'd ask myself, then quickly justify, *This will help them know how to deal with me.*

But the impulse only grew. Soon, I would talk about my educational accomplishments to whoever would listen. Finally, in desperation, I went back to God and asked for help. This voice, demanding attention before others because of my degree: it had gotten out of control.

God said, "Matt, give it to me." Now, being the spiritual giant that I am, I thought, "No way. You don't need this degree. I busted my butt to get it. It doesn't help You to have letters after Your name. *I* need it." But even as I protested, I knew: He was asking me to give it to Him in the sense of never using it for self-exaltation again. It was His—not mine anymore.

C. S. Lewis said it this way:

> The pleasure of pride is like the pleasure of scratching. If there is an itch one does want to scratch; but it is much nicer to have neither the itch nor the scratch. As long as we have the itch of self-regard we shall want the pleasure of self-approval; but the happiest moment are those when we forget our precious selves and have neither but have everything else (God, friends, animals, world) instead.[46]

---

[46] C. S. Lewis, *Letters of C. S. Lewis*, ed. W. H. Lewis (New York: Harcourt, Brace & World, Inc., 1966).

We focus on the outside. God works from the inside out whenever possible. He wants to capture the heart of each person first, developing the outworking of the heart to transform the thinking and actions of His children.

Pride, however, does the opposite. It focuses on the outward actions—the image—because that we can more easily control, and that is what others can see. What good does it do to have the right attitude if no one else can see it? Pride wants to only do things that others will notice (fear of man). Jesus, on the contrary, instructed us "not to let the right hand know what the left hand is doing."

Paul, writing to the church in Corinth, spoke of "those who take pride in appearance and not in heart."[47] Throughout Scripture, God reiterates that He cares for the true heart of things, not the outward appearance of them. "'Yet even now,' declares the LORD, 'Return to Me with all your heart, and with fasting, weeping and mourning; and rend your heart and not your garments.'"[48] This exposure of the heart is the very thing pride hates to do. We become vulnerable, under God's authority, exposed, powerless, and without the comfort of self-exaltation.

We are satisfied. When Israel entered the promised land, God gave them a clear warning:

---

[47] 2 Corinthians 5:12
[48] Joel 2:12-13

[W]hen you have eaten and are satisfied, and have built good houses and lived in them, and when your herds and your flocks multiply, and your silver and gold multiply, and all that you have multiplies, then your heart becomes proud, and you forget the LORD your God who brought you out from the land of Egypt, out of the house of slavery.[49]

Hosea writes later of this very thing: "As they had their pasture, they became satisfied, and being satisfied, their heart became proud; therefore they forgot Me."[50]

Something in our brokenness so longs for self-justification that when we reach a level of comfort and satisfaction, our pride wells up, and we think we have done it. We become convinced we got here by our wisdom and power, and we use it for self-exaltation: *I am good; I should be loved; I have the power within; I am somebody of importance.* It seems the thing to fear is not failure, but success.

Surprisingly, Scripture says this sort of pride was the primary sin of Sodom: "Behold, this was the guilt of your sister Sodom: she and her daughters had arrogance, abundant food, and careless ease, but she did not help the poor and needy."[51] The perversion and sin that we see as we read the story of Sodom all grew out of this area of pride unchecked.

---

[49] Deuteronomy 8:11-14

[50] Hosea 13:6

[51] Ezekiel 16:49

Summary

Humbling ourselves is not an option if we want the grace of God. Whatever we do, we will not be able to get around this humbling. To the degree you have humbled yourself here on earth, you will not be humbled in judgment. But to the degree you have not humbled yourself here, to that degree will you be humbled in judgment. Thank God, He does not stand over us in arrogance, demanding that we grovel. The very essence of humility, He comes down to walk alongside us, showing us how to do what He is asking, and inviting us to join Him.

If you are not walking intimately with others—if you experience jealousy, envy, strife, anger, competition, power, control, unbrokenness, or the fear of man in your habits and behavior—then it is time to ask for revelation of the root of pride at work in your life. Ask God for the grace you need to repent, to be broken, to change your heart and the way you think. Humble yourself before the Almighty God and choose life. Make Jesus your model.

How to do this?
- List the areas where you see pride in your life.
- List the people you have affected by it.
- Go to them and ask their forgiveness.
- Invite them to tell you when they see pride in your life.
- Begin to practice a new way of living.

Years ago, at the University of Edinburgh, Christian professor Stuart Blackie was presiding over his students' oral readings. One young man rose to begin his recitation, holding his book in his left hand rather than his right, as was the proper form. The professor thundered, "Take your book in your right hand, and be seated!"

The room echoed with his harsh rebuke. The student quietly held up his right arm—his arm ended at the wrist.

For a moment, Professor Blackie hesitated. Then left his podium. He walked through the rows to the student, put his arm around him, and wept openly. "I never knew about it," he said through his tears. "Please, will you forgive me?"

That young man later testified, "Professor Blackie led me to Christ. But he never could have done it if he had not made the wrong right."[52]

It is time to stand back from your life and your work: to gain a larger perspective of the work of God, and to look at the life you have lived. You have made poor choices in the past, as have others. But the time is now. What will you do when you get perspective and see the mess you have made?

---

[52] Source unknown.

CHAPTER FOUR

MOSES AND THE MESS HE MADE

Moses stood on the wall overlooking the city and watched its madness. Building projects were going on everywhere. People hurried around carrying baskets of sand and rocks. Rows of slaves pulled huge slabs of rock by long ropes. Lines of slaves carried supplies up the stairs of the buildings. Spread throughout the straining slaves, men with whips stood, carefully watching over the workers. Occasionally, the sound of a whip and a yell pierced the air as one of the workers made a mistake. The whip quickly brought them back into line.

As Moses watched, he felt the struggle within him. *Born and nursed by a Hebrew mother, adopted as a son of Pharaoh and educated in the best schools in Egypt, I have all the actions, knowledge, experiences and language of one people—and yet I seem to understand and have the heart of another.*

A snapping whip stirred him. *Am I Egyptian? Are my people beating the worthless slaves to build a great city and civilization—or am I Hebrew? Are my people oppressed by an unjust government that is using us and killing us to further its own pride?* He had asked himself this many times, and again, he had no answer. No choice seemed right. A prayer slowly rose from his lips: "Creator, show me who I am, that I might make the right choice."

...

"How many Hebrews does it take to build a city?" asked the Egyptian commander.

"I don't know, sir," replied the Hebrew slave.

"Maybe one less than we have here!" The man raised his whip and beat the Hebrew slave before him. "Stop relaxing, you lazy, worthless animal—get to work!"

The slave spit at the commander just as the whip came down.

Moses stood by and watched in horror. *That could as easily be me being beaten.* For a brief moment, something deeper than his education and childhood rose within him: an emotion he feared and yet longed for. He knew then that he was made in God's image. He could use his power and position to save his people.

The only difference between the slave on the ground and him was that his choice carried power. He could speak, and things would get done. He could define himself by his choice any way he desired. The slave, on the other hand, spoke and got beaten for it.

Moses looked around. No other Egyptians stood nearby. He ran to the Egyptian commander, grabbed the whip from him, and began beating him with the butt end. The man fell to the ground. All Moses' anger and fury seemed to flow from him. Every joke he had heard, every beating, seemed to explode out onto the man on the ground. Within minutes, Moses came to his senses and saw the commander lying dead before him.

Quickly, he dragged the commander out into the sand and buried him. No one had seen him, he was pretty certain. He glanced back at the beaten Hebrew slave, nodded his head, and walked away. It was done. He had made his choice. He was a Hebrew.

The next day, Moses heard a few people arguing. He stepped up to stop them, and they both turned on him. "Are you going to kill us like you did the commander?" said one of them. Moses stood and stared. Had the slave spread the story? Surely everyone knew what he had done by now.

That afternoon, one of the Egyptian commanders caught up to him, saying, "Moses, come quickly. Pharaoh summons you to the High Court."

Moses hesitated. That murder was his first conscious choice to identify with God and His people, to vent his anger at the injustice, and to try to help them. He had taken things into his own hands; he had used his power to help those afflicted. There would be a price for it.

If he showed up in court, he would be stripped of all power, probably killed. He knew that.

He did not look back but began to run. If by one choice he had created this mess, he could just as easily make another choice to get out of it. His choice was to run as far away as possible.

...

So what's in a choice?

Everything.

Let me explain. God spoke creation into existence. He said, "Let there be light," and there was light. God spoke and brought order out of chaos. With each new day, God spoke into existence a new element of creation. His spoken word created our world.

Everything around us that we can see, smell, taste, hear, or feel came about by God speaking it into existence—everything except us. When the Bible writes about us, it says, "Then the LORD God formed man of dust from the ground, and breathed into his nostrils the breath of life; and man became a living being."[53]

God did not speak us into existence. He formed the shell of man from the dust and then breathed into us the breath of life.

---

[53] Genesis 2:7

Take a breath and hold it. The air held inside of you is waiting for you to do something with it. What words will you form out of it? What will they express?

God made us in His image. He made us with the capacity to create. He gave us His breath and with it the freedom to finish creating with Him. God creates out of nothing: a feat far beyond us. We create out of His unspoken word, or breath, in us. Our choice is what forms and then finishes the breath of God in us. When we make a choice, we create something that never existed before. We take the breath of God and, with the power of our will, we create as He created, in our own small way.

What determines whether that choice is life-giving or destructive? It all comes down to whether we move towards joy, peace, faithfulness, intimacy, goodness, and love—or towards impurity, enmity, strife, jealousy, separation, and hatred. Simply put, it comes down to whether the choice is created in humility or pride. Our willingness to walk in humility or pride determines whether we create life or death.

The choice is ours.

...

When Moses finally slowed to a walk, a debate erupted in his mind with his conscience the prosecutor, and his own voice the defendant.

71

You killed a man. You are guilty.

He was just an Egyptian, Moses argued back. *He had killed many Hebrews before and would have killed that man if I had not intervened. I should be called a savior.*

His conscience pressed harder. *You murdered a man. You became angry and took your frustrations out on him. He beat the Hebrews to protect his people—you beat him to protect your people. You are no better than him.*

His mind objected, *It couldn't be helped. I had a position of authority to help my people, and that was my motive—to help them. That makes it right.*

You are trying to rationalize away the fact that you broke God's law. You are guilty of murder.

With that thought, Moses stopped. He knew he had no argument. He had studied the law and knew its vital importance to any kingdom. A kingdom's strength was only as strong as its law.

For the first time, Moses felt the heat of the sun beating down on him. *This desert... God has brought me out here to kill me as a murderer. I am no better than those who have raised me. God must feel about me the same way Pharaoh does. I deserve to die.* Should he even keep walking? He looked over his shoulder and all around. *Maybe I should just end it here and now—*

let the sun do its quick work. If the sun doesn't get me, God will use something else.

Fear gripped him again. He gazed into the relentless heat and the sand that seemed to go on forever. Finally he could stand it no more: he had to find a place to hide. He had to hide from the heat, Pharaoh—and God.

...

What is the worst that guilt produces when it is protected by pride?

Maybe you think the worst thing is how terrible you feel. Guilt hidden beneath pride takes away your peace and joy. It makes you insecure. It removes your capacity to love and opens the door to enmity and strife. It tempts you to hide.

Yes: all of these are true. These follow as natural consequences of a guilt that embraces pride. But they are not the most destructive.

The most destructive consequence of guilt shielded by pride is that it distorts our concept of God.

Why, you might ask, is our concept of God so important?

"What comes into our minds when we think about God is the most important thing about us," writes A.

W. Tozer. "We tend by a secret law of the soul to move toward our mental image of God." That image will either draw us toward Him or repel us from Him. No individual or group has ever been greater than its concept of God.

Imagine a crime scene, with police questioning witnesses. One of them actually saw who committed the murder, and so the police bring in an artist. The witness describes the perpetrator, and the artist draws a picture based on that description. All those involved in the case will use this picture to track down the killer. The closer this picture is to the real person, the easier it will be to find the person.

In the same way, the closer our concept of God is to reality, the easier He will be to find.

Pride is a false witness. It gives a wrong description of God, knowing that if our guilt is exposed, we become vulnerable. We imagine that God will deal severely with us, and that is too much to bear. If we have done something that we know God must hate, we plunge into fear: by all rights, the one, the only one, whose love we need and crave should be angry at us, and we can do nothing about it.

Guilt produces fear. Fear seeks a way to self-justify. Self-justification opens the door to illusions and deception. We know we deserve the penalty, yet we don't want to be punished. So our pride tries to create a way that will explain away our guilt or somehow get us out from under the judge's eye. It does this by changing our perception of who God is:

God is too busy to be concerned with my little life.

God is distant and removed, in a far-off place called heaven.

God doesn't really have a moral law.

Even if there is a moral law, it's not set in stone: it's just suggestions, good ideas, to help guide us.

God is love; He will overlook my mistakes.

I have done enough good to offset the bad I have done.

A good God can't be angry for that long. He will get over it.

God is not big enough to see the specifics of what I am doing.

Yeah, right. All these are illusions—lies—deceptions created for one purpose and one purpose alone: to protect our guilty choices from being exposed. We don't want to be found out and will do anything to protect ourselves.

Yet a god created in the depths of a fallen mind will bear little resemblance to the Almighty God as He is in all His majesty and glory.[54]

...

Moses found a place to hide and sat down on a shade-cooled rock. He shuddered, remembering the look in the Egyptian's eyes as his life slowly slipped away. For the first time, Moses realized he had not even felt sorry about killing the man. He would have killed many more if he thought he could have gotten away with it.

I have chosen to be angry for many years, he thought. *I have chosen to hate them for oppressing the people. My people. I have chosen to hate myself for not doing anything to help them. I have chosen to love power and pleasure more than justice and truth.*

I have become an angry, bitter, power-hungry, controlling, murdering man.

Something new was born in him that day. The seeds of humility were planted deep in Moses' heart as he accepted the reality of who he had become. Watered with the pain of reality, the hardened soil of his life that would before have killed any new seeds now lay soft

---

[54] Adapted from A. W. Tozer, *Knowledge of the Holy* (New York: Harper Collins, 1961).

and ready for growth. Humility never grows in the soil of illusions, blindness, or deceit. The seeds of humility can only grow in the rich soil of reality.

Moses waited in the shade until evening and then pushed on. Traveling at night was much easier and would probably save his life. He walked long and hard into the night and just before morning decided to lie down. Sleep came quickly.

He rose in the new light of day and looked around him in amazement. He did not recognize anything around him. Soon he spotted a well not too far off. Marveling at his good luck, he drew some water to drink deeply, washed his face, and then sat on the edge to develop a plan for the day.

As he sat to ponder, the sound of sheep stirred him to movement. He stood to see a small group of sheep and goats coming to the well, attended by—he counted—seven shepherds, all of them women. He sat and watched as they worked around him.

They did not want to bother this strange-looking Egyptian sitting on the well. "Hurry up," said one shepherd. "The others will be coming soon and we must finish before they get here, or we'll be here all morning waiting for them to finish. Hurry!" She drew water up and filled the trough.

The sound of more sheep and goats soon filled the air as other shepherds began to arrive. These men laughed at the women and pushed them aside. They hit the drinking sheep with their staffs and chased them away. "You women must learn your place," one of them declared. "Let us take care of our herd first and you can then do as you will."

The men paid little attention to the extravagantly dressed Egyptian sitting and watching—until he stood and challenged them in their own language. "Let the women take their share," he said. "They were here first. You can push a group of women around. Let's see what you can do with a man."

The men took a step back. This man's voice held a strange authority, mixed with anger, as if he were looking for a fight. They had a long day ahead of them and were not prepared for this.

Moses called the seven women forward with their sheep and goats and began pulling water from the well. He filled the trough over and over until they had all they needed to drink. They slowly began to move off. Moses then moved a short distance away and sat on a rock to watch the other shepherds.

Once the men had watered their flock, they left. Moses sat pondering what to do next. He was in no hurry; he did not know where he would find water again.

After a while, several of the women shepherds came back and found Moses sitting there. They said,

"Stranger, you have helped us. We are sorry we did not help you. Do you have a place to stay?"

"No, I don't," he said.

"Then come and stay with us. We can give you food and rest."

"Thank you," Moses said as he stood to walk with them. *I will be with the women taking care of sheep. A prince of Egypt, sunk to this.* Moses shook his head as he followed the women. With no place to go or people of his own, he quickly took on the dress and customs of the land. They made a place for him among them. As time passed, he married and settled among them as a shepherd.

...

Moses carried his anger with him wherever he went. In his early years as a shepherd, he would throw rocks or beat the shrubs. The heat quickly proved stronger than he, so at last he settled for shouting.

One day, Moses looked bleakly at the barrenness around him: no one but his sheep for miles. He lifted his voice, looked to the heavens, and cried out, "Why, God? Why do You take such pleasure in humiliating me?"

Silence hung in the air as Moses waited.

"Not a day goes by that You do not find new ways to humble me. You crush me like a bug underfoot. Why?"

He breathed in, trying to relax. When he finally quieted himself, he heard God speak: "Moses, I AM the most humble being in the universe. I take no pleasure in the pain of your humility—only in its fruit, that we might have a relationship. I humble Myself to be with you, and only by walking in humility can you join Me."

...

Moses lay on his mat, so thin it provided little comfort from the hard ground. Eventually he drifted off to sleep and dreamed. Images came to his mind, images lifted from many parts of his life.

He saw himself, dressed in the finest clothes in the land, standing before a bronze mirror and staring at his reflection. A voice whispered, "You have chosen pride." In shattering revelation, Moses saw his heart. He felt he was better than anyone else in the land. Pride.

In his dream, Moses saw himself before his teacher, caught in a lie. He heard himself protesting, "I did not lie. I never make mistakes. Mistakes are weakness, and I'm not weak." The voice again whispered, "You have

CHOSEN PRIDE," and the illusion fell away to reveal a deceitful heart: he would not admit his mistakes. Pride.

Moses saw himself in the shade, standing and watching the Hebrews being beaten day after day. Thousands of days passed, and yet he continued to watch the people beaten and killed, doing nothing. Again the voice whispered, "YOU HAVE CHOSEN PRIDE." He had hardened his heart and made excuses for years. Pride.

More images rushed in, and the verdict became clear.

You have more fear of man than fear of Me.

You are unteachable.

"YOU HAVE CHOSEN PRIDE."

You are full of self-pity.

You are angry and impatient.

"YOU HAVE CHOSEN PRIDE."

You think you earned your status.

You have blamed everyone else for your problems.

You are jealous of others and cannot enjoy anyone else's success.

"YOU HAVE CHOSEN PRIDE."

Moses awoke, sat up, and put his hand over his

heart. It beat wildly, but that was all. Just a dream. He lay back down, looked around the small tent, and saw the last flames from the fire outside dancing on a log. He mumbled to himself, "I can no longer be proud. I have lost it all. I have nothing left. At least the pride has gone with it."

Out on a lonely desert mountain, in an old tent with few possessions, on a mat on a hard floor, hiding for his life, Moses mouthed the words through his graying beard: "I have chosen pride." He realized then that he was the most arrogant man in the world.

...

Days and then weeks passed. Memories slowly bubbled to the surface and came alive, reminding him daily of his pride. A word harshly spoken; an indolent air, not bothering to give the scraps off his table to the starving; sipping water in front of the thirsty and then pouring it out in the sand as they watched; his loud and arrogant boasting at the feasts thrown for him...

With each fresh revelation of the depth of his pride, Moses wept and called out to God. If anyone had come near, they would have heard him burst out in anguished tones:

"Oh, if only I could go back and undo it."

"How can I show my sorrow?"

"I am a fool."

"I deserve to die."

"I'm sorry. I had no idea my heart was so corrupt."

"You put me in a position to help the people, and I wasted it on my own desires and lusts."

"I could see no one but myself. I was consumed with my own interests."

He knew that his pride separated him from his Creator. His pride had destroyed his life. He could blame no one but himself.

What can I do to make up for it? Moses thought of all the things he could do to show his remorse. He could fast, beat his body into submission, spend hours in prayer, give his few meager possessions away… His mind wrestled with any options he could think of. *Do I offer sacrifices, thousands of rams, ten thousand rivers of oil, my own son?* When he could bear the weight of what he owed to God no more, he called out to Him, "What do You require of me?"

"Do justice, love mercy, and walk humbly with your God," the voice whispered.[55]

He let the words sink in.

---

[55] Taken from Micah 6:8

He wanted to give or do so many things. Then a new revelation struck him. Everything he wanted to give would be his attempt to earn God's love, to prove how loveable, how good, he was: more pride. *I am not good. I am not loveable because of what I have done, and yet You love me.*

Moses made the most humbling choice one could make. He let the Creator of the universe, the Almighty God, love him when he knew he was not loveable. He chose to receive with thankfulness that which he hadn't earned and yet desperately needed. What could be more humbling than that?

...

Life is full of many different choices. What clothes to wear, what food to eat, where you work, or who you marry. Each day bursts with choices, but in the midst of them all, don't be fooled. As it was for Moses, so it is for us. Only one choice matters. All other choices are a by-product of this one choice:

The choice to humble ourselves and receive God's love.

Moses humbled himself and let God love him as he was. He would not embrace the illusion of fine clothes and abundant food. He would not seek power. He would not trust his education. He would not embrace the security of an already-established nation. He would not seek to justify himself.

One choice, and yet the epicenter of every choice. We make a choice to go on a trip, and each choice from then on reinforces the first choice we made to get started. So with our choice to humble ourselves. We make a choice that embraces humility as the foundation for all our choices. This choice, made often enough, forms our habits. These habits form our character.

Our character determines our destiny.

...

Sometimes the most humble choice is the small one made in faithfulness day after day, week after week, year after year, decade after decade. Nothing courageous. Nothing fancy. No one looking on. Feeling the pain of insignificance with the heavens seeming as hard as brass.

Moses rose and looked out over the harsh land before him, listening to the sound of his small herd of sheep bleating, calling him to take them to the pasture. The choice again confronted him.

He thought of the day ahead and could foresee it as though he had already lived it—as indeed he had, for each day seemed like the last. The heat would come and beat on him all day. He would keep trying to find shade as it constantly eluded him. His eyes would ache from trying to look through the heat waves for a few bushes to feed his flock. He would strive to maintain the ongoing watchfulness required to make sure each of the animals did not wander off.

The taste and grit of dust his constant companion.

The thorns and needles scraping against him and sometimes piercing his flesh, that weakest of armors against them.

The solitary places and loneliness, sometimes going for days without hearing a word spoken by another human being.

The daily stupidity of the sheep a source of anger, ongoing anxiety, and even crazy laughter when nothing else worked.

Each day, it was the same. Today would be no different.

As he often did, Moses spoke to the sheep to find comfort. "I have told you before, but I know you want to hear it again," he said to one of the nearest. "I was once one of the most powerful men in Egypt. You should be honored to have me to watch over you. Did you know I can read and speak different languages? Did you know I could organize a whole city with my eyes closed and still have time for long luxurious meals?"

Silence followed. A familiar *baa* arose from one and then another sheep. "I know. You are not impressed. I am not impressed either."

A loud *baa* silenced Moses as he listened. Something was wrong. He quickly walked over to the narrow gully and looked down into it. There at the bottom, stuck between two rocks, was Ishpo.

"You've done it again!" Moses' laugh echoed in the small gully as he began the climb down. "This is the third time this week. You are teaching me much." Moses reached down with his rod and with the curved end pulled Ishpo up and out. Ishpo struggled and finally jumped free to scamper up the rocks and join the flock.

The heat of the sun breaking up the shade pushed Moses out to find a new spot. As he stepped over a rock, he tripped and fell. He turned angrily to face the rock, catching himself quickly lest anyone, approaching by rare chance, see him down. Suddenly he laughed at himself. *My sheep are smarter than I,* he thought. *They get stuck and accept it as an expression of their own limitations. They are not embarrassed; they just call for help. Yet when I fall with no one around to see me, my pride flares up. I refuse to make a mistake or be weak. I assume I should know all things and never trip and fall, or even admit I don't know.* The thought struck him much harder than the fall.

Finally, he said out loud, "I am human." He reached down, fisted some dirt, and said, "This is my heritage: that from which I was brought forth and to which I will return." Everything around him spoke of weakness and limitations. The sun beat down on him: too long in it and he was gone. His limited supply of food. The sheep that seemed to reveal the limits of any intelligence.

He let his hand drop and the dirt fall back to the ground. He called out, "Come, my little ones. We must keep moving."

CHAPTER FIVE

MOSES AND HUMILITY AS A SAINT

*[T]housands of humans have been brought to think that hu-
mility means pretty women trying to believe they are ugly and
clever men trying to believe they are fools... [God] wants to
bring the man to a state of mind in which he could design the
best cathedral in the world, and know it to be the best, and
rejoice in the fact, without being any more (or less) or otherwise glad at having done it than he would be if it had been
done by another. [God] wants him, in the end, to be so free
from any bias in his own favor that he can rejoice in his own
talents as frankly and gratefully as in his neighbor's talents—
or in a sunrise, an elephant, or a waterfall... He wants to kill
their animal self-love as soon as possible; but it is His long-
term policy... to restore to them a new kind of self-love—a
charity and gratitude for all selves, including their own.*
C. S. Lewis, The Screwtape Letters

God did not break up the soil of Moses' hard, arrogant heart just to watch him die in isolation in the
desert. Forty years in the desert made for a long, painful preparation, but make no mistake: God used each
moment to prepare the soil of Moses' heart for a great
and mighty work, one in which Moses would both receive life himself and bring forth great life for others.

...

Choices made over the years create a pattern that reveals our view of ourselves and of the world. A thought made manifest becomes a choice; the choice takes action, forming a habit; habits establish our character; and character, once fully formed, determines our destiny. As the popular saying goes, ideas have consequences.

One day, like so many others, Moses was pasturing his flock. He led the sheep to a hidden part of the wilderness, a place called Horeb, the mountain of God.

As he moved up the mountain, he hesitated and stared up ahead. He could see a bush on fire. He'd wait for the fire to quickly consume the bush before taking his sheep past the spot. It was rare, but not impossible, for a tree to burst into flame in this intense heat. Usually the fires died shortly after they began. His sheep began to bleat behind him as he waited and waited. To his amazement, the bush went on burning, unconsumed.

Curious, Moses led his sheep to a small grazing area nearby and then went to investigate. When God saw that Moses turned aside to see the bush, He called to him, "Moses, Moses!"

"Here I am," Moses responded.

"Remove your sandals from your feet, for the place on which you are standing is holy ground."

Moses was terrified. Thoughts flooded his mind. *I stand on holy ground, and yet I am not holy. Like a bug, circling the light of a fire, getting too close, and finally being consumed by it, I will surely be consumed by God.*

The choice that confronted him would be one of the most difficult choices of his life. Would he submit to a holiness not his own? Would he acknowledge that there existed a holiness far greater, far richer, far purer than anything he had ever dreamed? To admit there was a standard of purity in the universe would be to seal his own fate; he knew he did not measure up. He knew it would be much easier to make the choice to run than to submit.

Instead, Moses removed his sandals and chose God's perspective. That choice formed the foundation of the man he would become. With his choice to take God's side, God revealed His heart to Moses and told him of the cries of Israel for help, their affliction, their suffering, and how God had heard these cries and would provide deliverance.

God then said these terrifying words: "Therefore, come now, and I will send you to Pharaoh, so that you may bring My people, the sons of Israel, out of Egypt."

Thoughts began to flood Moses' mind. *I am a simple shepherd. I can barely handle the sheep. I already tried to help the people, and they didn't want my help. I am a wanted man. Pharaoh will kill me.* He finally responded, "Who am I, that I should go to Pharaoh, and that I should bring the sons of Israel out of Egypt?"

"I will be with you, Moses."

"I have no power. How can I do anything?"

"What do you have in your hand, Moses?"

"A staff."

"Throw it on the ground."

Moses dropped it. The staff became a serpent. Moses turned and began to run.

"Moses, pick it up."

Moses stopped, turned slowly, and looked at the serpent. It hissed at him. Then he reached out his hand to pick it up.

...

What do you have in your hand?

Such a simple question, yet so foundational to understanding the gifts He has given us. And that question leads to two more: will you use it? And if you do, for whose purposes?

A stick used by a shepherd is called a staff or a rod. Moses' staff was simply a branch broken off some dying tree; he had used it for years. The power lay not in the stick but in the attitude of the one using it. Moses had had his own attitude back in Egypt; he thought he could use his own gifts, his power, his anger, to bring about justice on his own. God challenged him now to a different attitude: obedient humility, birthed in faith that God Himself would bring about the victory.

A gift humbly expressed in the light moves us towards Holiness.

Can I use the words *humble* and *holy* in the same sentence? I must confess, they do not always fit together in my thinking. Let me borrow an illustration from C. S. Lewis:

> Imagine a lot of people who have always lived in the dark. You come and try to describe to them what light is like. You might tell them that if they come into the light that same light would fall on them all and they would all reflect it and thus become what we call visible. Is it not quite possible that they would imagine that, since they were all receiving the same light, and all reacting to it in the same way (i.e. all reflecting it), they would all look alike? Whereas you and I know that the light will in fact bring out, or show up, how different they are. [56]

I often think of holiness in the same way: when it falls on me, I will be the same as everyone else. I will be a religious clone with no uniqueness or beauty that is my own unique expression of Him. A foolish thought, as foolish as the thought that light shining where once darkness flourished would reveal nothing but sameness.

[56] C. S. Lewis, *Mere Christianity*.

Humility recognizes and embraces what something is. Holiness reveals what it could be and was made to be. In humility, I embrace what the light reveals, that unique expression of God in me (in us), and I look for ways to walk that out. I don't have to fear the light if I am willing to walk into what it exposes.

As light exposes a diverse world in all its beauty, so Holiness reveals who God is and how far above our humble view of reality He is. It is both our terror and our joy if we will humble ourselves and embrace Him. Our choice can birth His beauty through us.

...

Although we use our gifts and callings through action, in their purest sense, they are something that we *are*. God has taken a part of Himself and put it in us—not the whole, only a part, but a part of the Almighty God and no less. He gives it freely and will not take it back. Moses' life bears witness to this, in his service to his people, and his calling to deliver others from oppression.

The first recorded example is of him killing the Egyptian, trying to help the Israelites. Deep within himself, he knew that he had a part to play in delivering his people. The act of murder was the misuse of his gift: his attempt to deliver the people in his own strength and his own way.

Just a short time later we can see it again. Moses, running for his life, ends up at a well observing the tableau of male shepherds bullying female shepherds. He defends the women from the other shepherds and helps them water their sheep.

In one situation, his gift got him in serious trouble, forcing him to flee for his life. In the next situation, it won him a home. What made the difference?

His relationship with God through humility.

When Moses did not do things in his own strength and power—when he did not do things his own way—when he dealt with the pride of his heart, then he could truly express the gift of God through God's power. As with Moses, so with us: when we grow to be like God and model Him in His humility, His gift becomes more real within us.

...

Some choices come easily, rising from within us and flowing forth like a stream. Others are more difficult. We know they will come with a great price tag attached. For Moses, confronting the people who had raised and loved him was that more difficult choice.

Moses stood in fear and trembling, knowing the pride of the powerful and the power of those with dark magic. He knew who he was: a murderer, a sheep herd-er with a staff in hand and a brother by his side, a young man raised in the very courts he would now challenge. But he also knew he was a man with a choice—the most powerful tool in the universe when aligned with the Almighty God.

If only he had one single choice to make, once and done, and he could go home! But it wasn't that simple. He had to make a choice and bear the consequenc-es. No-one living in darkness likes to be confronted by someone living in the light. Especially when that someone is the descendant of a man who saved them from famine, and whose descendants they forced into slavery.

With each choice the conflict rose.

Pharaoh stated, "Your choice to turn a rod into a snake is no greater than my magicians."

"Your choice to turn the Nile into blood is still no greater than my magicians."

"So you do have power that my magicians don't have. Let's see you use it to help your people make bricks with no straw."

I don't know about you, but I would have probably given up. Those Moses had come to save had turned against him because he only made things harder. They didn't want more problems. They just wanted a simple way out: a gift given that would remove all their struggles.

Moses humbled himself with each choice and the resulting conflict. He reminded himself that God had a plan, and it depended on Moses' choice, not Moses' power. Each day he confronted those in power and stood by his choice. He was not such a fool as to think that freedom came at no cost, or even that life came without conflict.

...

Moses stood on the edge of the sea and looked out. Behind him, he could feel the heat of the fire separating him and the Israelites from the rabid Egyptian forces who desperately wanted to kill them all. *No going back now,* he thought with a sigh. *We wouldn't exactly be welcomed.*

Moses knew where God wanted them to go, but how would they get there? Pressure built within him. *What do I do?* They had no ships. They couldn't swim. Moses looked at the young children clinging to their parents, and the older people supporting themselves with walking sticks.

Then he looked at the staff in his hand. Suddenly he saw, in his mind's eye, the tree from which he had cut this staff on when he first started caring for the sheep.

He remembered his first thought: *Just like me, a little bent, gnarly knots here and there, attached to a once great but now very dead tree, alone, of no use.* He felt compelled to take it and make it his own.

He remembered when this same rod became a snake in the courts of Pharaoh, eating the snakes Pharaoh's magicians had conjured. Then the plagues. He had held up an old, gnarly, dead stick and brought Egypt to its knees. The river turned to blood. The darkness, gnats, hailstones… all of it came when he prayed and lifted up the dead, useless stick.

It had never worn out. In all the years of walking and using it for untold purposes, it had never worn out.

You are that stick, he heard God's voice speak within him. *You were useless, bent, and gnarled, stuck in a dead nation, and I have pulled you out. In My hand, you never wear out.*

Revelation washed over Moses. He saw the pride of his heart in thinking the miracles were his, something he had to create by an act of his will, that somehow his choices would save the people. The image of the Egyptian that he killed tormented him again. His choices in his strength to save a nation didn't help.

Moses looked at his hand's well-worn place on his staff, the comfortable grip. God whispered to him, *As your hand fits on the staff and has used it, so My hand fits on your life, and I will use it. Stand and see the Glory of God, for it is not your choice but Mine that will save the people.*

Moses stood and stared at the waters as a strong image began to grow in his mind. He looked at his hand on the rod and then walked out into the water. He turned to face the people staring at him, shaking their heads, whispering: "We can't swim. We'll never make it."

Slowly, Moses held up the rod of God.

A loud rushing sound filled the air as the people cowered and held each other. The wind pushed back the waters, and a way through the sea emerged. God had chosen His way to save His people.

Humility as Saints

Henry Augustus Rowland, professor of physics at Johns Hopkins University, was once called as an expert witness at a trial. During cross-examination, a lawyer demanded, "What are your qualifications as an expert witness in this case?"

The normally modest and retiring professor replied quietly, "I am the greatest living expert on the subject under discussion."

Later, a friend well acquainted with Rowland's disposition expressed surprise at the professor's uncharacteristic answer. Rowland answered, "Well, what did you expect me to do? I was under oath."[57]

We think humility means never doing things well, or never admitting that we do things well. I grew up with a dad, older brother, and older sister who all had very strong personalities. I was more like Mom in that I tended to be naturally quiet and withdrawn. In order to survive in the family, I decided it was easier to not say anything and not compete with the others. As I grew older, I discovered a talent at sports my brother did not share. My dad loved this in me, and I could see the pain in my brother because of it. In my little mind, I thought that my brother's pain was my fault. Something in me shut down; I didn't want to exhibit skill, for surely it would cause pain in others just as my sports skill caused pain in my brother.

Early in my Christian walk, I figured God was like my dad. If I succeeded spiritually, I would cause pain in others, because God would get greater joy out of me than them. Only as I studied humility did I discover a God in this way, unlike my father—a God who made me who I am—an impartial God, one who doesn't love me because I do life well or poorly but simply loves me, no matter what. I can express any gifts God has given me, giving them back to God as a living sacrifice,

---

[57] *Today in the Word*, August 5, 1993.

and let it go at that. God can figure out what He wants to do with it.

...

In Innsbruck, Austria at the 1964 Olympic two-man bobsled competition, a British team driven by Tony Nash stood in second place when they realized, with sinking hearts, that they had broken a bolt on the rear axle of their sled. The mishap would put them out of the running entirely.

Eugenio Monti, the celebrated Italian bobsled driver, finished his own run in first place, and then he heard of the misfortune that had visited the British team. Immediately, Monti took the bolt from his sled's rear axle and sent it to the top of the hill. With it, the British team completed their run and won the gold medal. Monti's team took bronze.

People raved about Monti's selfless display of sportsmanship. But Monti simply replied, "Tony Nash did not win because I gave him a bolt. Tony Nash won because he was the best driver."[58]

He wasn't arrogant, trying to win at any cost. He gave it his best, and that satisfied him. He was a winner in God's eyes.

---

[58] Paraphrased from SPIN Magazine, February 2002.

I must confess: I have often struggled with comparison. When I look at myself, my gifts seem so small and insignificant when valued against the gifts of others. Over the last years, I have often turned to the story in the Gospels of the widow's mite.[59] Jesus watches the people lining up to give their offerings to God; I imagine the heavy sound of gold dropped by hands eager to impress God. Then a widow brings two pennies. To her horror, Jesus calls the disciples to Himself, looking right at her. Surely now they will mock her small gift! Perhaps she tries to get away but cannot press through the crowds gathering to see what Jesus will say.

Then, to her absolute amazement, He says that she has put in more than all the others combined. Jesus judges by a completely different standard. He does not judge by comparative size or importance, but by whether it is a sacrifice of love as an expression of the heart.

Jesus tells us that even a cup of water given as an expression of His love through us will not go unnoticed by Him, whether you have a gift or many gifts. If they are in hospitality, giving, or serving—whether your ministry includes miracles or comforting the sick and dying—whether you start new ministries—whether you do church work or are called to business, government work, engineering, medicine, or teaching—whatever the gift(s), you must embrace it and let it be just

---

[59] Luke 21:1

that. Like two pennies in the hand of an old widow, something given from the heart gives God great pleasure and will not go unnoticed by Him.

You may be tempted to think that if you have accepted your limitations, if you have dealt with your pride, then you are walking in humility. In reality, the first two expressions of humility (humility as creation and as a sinner) merely prepare us for the purest form of humility. The greatest joy of humility is the choice made to express God's goodness in your own unique way: not comparing yourself with others, nor measuring your value by how far you surpass others, but simply letting the Spirit of the living God infuse your life and touch the world around you.

God's goal in humbling us does not stop at showing us our limitations and weaknesses and calling us to repent of our sin. No, He uses these methods only as a means to what is on His heart. Imagine God as a farmer, searching night and day until He finds the right field, painstakingly removing all of its stones and weeds, and then plowing the soil to break up its hardness. Would He stop there, satisfied that He had cleansed and broken the land?

The goal for the land is to *produce*—to bring forth life to bless others. God uses humility to prepare the soil of our hearts to release the gifts that He plants within us. And He does all this not to break us down or bring us low, but that we might produce life, experiencing blessing ourselves and blessing others.

You begin by humbling yourself and embracing the fact that you are made in God's image, that you have a gift resident in you, and that He loves it when in humility you give it to others. Begin today. Be who God has made you to be. Humble yourself, and let Him flow through you in an expression of love and joy: the gift of God given back to God.

...

Humility as a saint grew in Moses as he made more and more choices to humble himself before God—not pretending he had no gifts, but also not caring that his gifts be better or more important than those of others. Years after the parting of the Red Sea, Joshua approached Moses with concerns about people prophesying in the camp. He told Moses to put a stop to it, but instead, Moses said to Joshua, "Are you jealous for my sake? Would that all the Lord's people were prophets, that the Lord would put His Spirit upon them!"[60] Moses did not think of protecting his own importance or uniqueness. He cared only to see God at work in their midst. Humility as a saint came like a reflex to him, after constant, years-long choosing of it.

[60] Numbers 11:29

Choices often seem as small as a drop of water. On their own, seen in the light of the brief moment, they do not seem to result in much. But have you ever seen a place where a drop of water fell repeatedly, persistently, continually, over and over again? Stalactites and stalagmites are built one drop at a time. Valleys take shape from millions of drops of water that join together and run towards the sea. So it is with our choices. Alone, they have little force, but when seen in the light of time, they have a long-term impact. They are the stuff that changes the landscape of our world.

Israel made choices for 400 years. They had strongly set patterns that would prove difficult to change. This can work for good or evil. An entire community of people will build, as it were, a collection of choices, like the rivers formed by millions of droplets. The body of Christ operates in this way as well. God promises, "And if My people who are called by My name will humble themselves and pray and seek My face and turn from their wicked ways, then I will hear from heaven, will forgive their sin and will heal their land."[61]

So the question is, will our collective choice be for humility?

---

[61] 2 Chronicles 7:14

CHAPTER SIX

MYTHS ABOUT HUMILITY

In order for any worldview to make sense, it must answer three primary questions.

1) Who am I? or, Where did we come from?
2) What has gone wrong with the world?
3) What can we do to fix it?

Humility is the beginning point for answering these questions:

1) We are finite and limited creatures made by God in His own image.
2) We have chosen to defy God and rebel from Him, which has broken our world away from God's original plan.
3) Only as we understand and embrace humility (including our gifts) will we truly see life restored to ourselves, the world, and the relationships around us.

To discover counterfeit bills, experts study real bills minutely, training themselves to recognize the fake by knowing the true thing by heart. This is why we have taken the time to understand each of the three areas of humility. With humility, there are clearly counterfeits out there—beliefs about what humility means that imitate but twist the truth—and now that we have studied the true picture, I want to expose some of the more common counterfeits. These counterfeits reveal how deeply interconnected the three aspects of humility are, and how we must embrace all three to walk fully in the grace of God.

Humility entails lesser value. One of the most damaging religious ideas out there is the idea that to truly humble yourself, you must remove all value from yourself. You aim to care about nothing, have no talents or praiseworthy qualities, and deflect attention to the extent that you cease to exist, as it were. This total self-annihilation is a form of religious suicide, and one that much more closely resembles certain strains of Eastern Hinduism rather than Christianity. God does call us to lay down our lives as a gift back to Him, to break the heart of selfishness and let His life flow through us. But if we build this healthy response on a foundation of misconceived humility, we will not find grace.

Understanding humility this way often leads to hating the gift God has put in us. We think every talent or good quality in us is pride and therefore sin, like an artist gifted in drawing or painting. She longs from God to express it but feels condemned, trying to repent of the gift in her. Many people spend their lives torn like this, wanting to express God in them, yet still under the pain of a fallen family, culture, or even church that can't see the gift as God does.

God settles our value. He and He alone determines what we are worth and how we are to live. He has declared our value to Him, not because of anything we have done, but because He is love and cares for us. Humility accepts that value as a gift from God and walks in it.

Humility of creation is important here, otherwise we would think any gift has to be perfect every time we use it, and complete so that we need not lean on others. But knowing we are limited and finite means our gift is subject to these aspects as well. I need the wisdom of others to fully use my gift, and when I do so, I need not agonize over mistakes, knowing that even with the gifts God has given me, I am weak and still learning how to express them.

Humility just means being weak and vulnerable. In a sense this is true, but it is not the complete picture of humility, for we are also made in God's image. Somehow, He took a piece of Himself and planted it in each of us. I may be a tiny collection of dust living on an insignificant planet, but I am also made in the image of God with a piece of Him resident in me, waiting to be called upon and expressed in the power of the Holy Spirit. Being weak and fragile doesn't translate automatically into insignificance or meaninglessness.

Another pitfall of this thinking happens when people humiliated by their weaknesses think that because they have been humiliated, they have repented. How many people sit in church today because they found themselves helpless and in trouble? Maybe one man got into an accident, feared for his life, and called out to God. Maybe one woman despaired at her failing business and came to God from desperation. Maybe chronic sickness brought another to the church door. These people, confronted with their mortality and weakness, know they need help and try to strike a deal with God: "Okay God, if you help me, I will go to church and do what you want." God reaches out to them because He responds to humility, and they end up in church.

Sometimes stories like this lead to life and fruitfulness—but only if the people go beyond just admitting their limitations. If they don't, they think this is repentance and they can sit back and enjoy the rest of the ride. They are sadly mistaken. Their initial humility did not birth true humility, and unless they continue towards God, they may eventually lose that relationship, or (at best) the relationship will grow cold and stale. A partial birth is not a true birth.

We only need humility when we sin. Some people go as far as to say that we *need* sin to keep us humble. It is not sin that truly humbles us, but grace. We know what we deserve, but when we get love that we don't deserve, it overwhelms and humbles us. Humility clearly includes dealing with sin, but even after a million years in heaven, we will need humility to walk with God.

If humility were only linked to sin, then the moment we left sin behind, we would no longer need humility. If this were true, then God is not humble, because He has never chosen sin. But humility entails more than repentance from sin. We will always be God's creation and His saints, and we will therefore always need humility as the expression of our limitations and the gift of God within us.

Closely related to this is the idea that any mistake, even losing one's car keys or mistakenly giving the wrong answer to a question, comes from sin; we think when we are truly humble, we will never make mistakes or never have problems. Again, this is a huge misunderstanding of humility at work in us and a forgetfulness of humility as creation. A perfectly holy and humble person who has repented of all sin will still make mistakes, assume things that are wrong, trip and fall, or simply need to ask questions. These do not come as the result of sin. They are just the expression of a finite human being who embraces weakness as a part of life.

Humility is a mystical, spiritual event that just happens to us. Sometimes we remove humility from the physical world and make it a mystical event that God does in us, one in which we have no choice. We consider it a blessing that only God can give, and He seems to only want to give it to a few of us. Fortunately, that lets me off the hook. If it's God's job to "do" humility to me, then I don't have any responsibility to work at it.

Yes, God gives us grace that humbles us, but we *do* have a choice. God made the material world and called it good. He wants to be involved in all aspects of life with us. Deuteronomy speaks of God humbling the people by letting them be hungry: using the material world to test and refine them so that they might mature and be more like God.[62] Humility came in their choice and how they responded to the challenges they faced in the material world. As with them, so with us: humility must be a conscious choice over the years, not something we wait for until it happens to us.

Humility means feeling bad about myself. In our fallen world, we will have times of insecurity, of feeling bad about ourselves, of experiencing guilt and shame; but these feelings, while they can be used by God to bring us into humility, are not by themselves true indicators of humility. Humility comes from the choices we make: how we respond to those feelings in light of who God is and who He made us to be. True humility, in the end, is at work when our focus is not on ourselves.

We can be humble towards God and not man. This is a lie right from the pit of hell. We get this idea from religion. Like the Pharisees, we only believe this if we use our religion to make us feel better about ourselves and better than others. Then our humility becomes pride: a platform to exalt ourselves over others. True

---

[62] Deuteronomy 8:3

humility appears in every relationship, or it is not there at all.

If God has blessed me with talent, I don't need to be humble about it. We sometimes attempt to compartmentalize humility, to keep it in the realm of "spiritual" things and not bring it into the realm of our daily life and gifts. Imagine a man gifted with great oratory skills. If he limits humility to matters of sin and does not understand humility as a saint, he could misinterpret God's gift at work in him as God's contentment with him—God's approval of the current state of his heart. He does not realize that God's gift of fine oration will be at work in him whether he submits it to God or not. Even walking in pride, the gift will still work. His gift might even bless others and earn their praise, and he could be tempted to think God doesn't care about the man's prideful state—a dangerous assumption that in the end will bring him trouble and loss in relationships. In God's eyes, such a man would not be successful.

James writes about this when he says that "the rich man is to glory in his humiliation, because like flowering grass he will pass away."[63] If your gift allows you to make money, great! Just remember, you are dust and will return to dust, and you can't take any of it with you. The gift belongs to God and must be given back to him in humility, not exulted in through pride, as though we ourselves made our gifts.

[63] James 1:10

The freedom repentance gives us here—the freedom of rejecting pride in giftedness and instead walking in humble giftedness—comes through knowing that our gift doesn't make us more or less special in God's eyes. We are all sinners saved by grace and adopted into God's family.

You can see this combination of humility in David's life in the Old Testament. He had wonderful gifts in worship and warfare. A brilliant strategist who knew how to work with people, he grew to become king over the nation. When bringing in the ark of the Lord into the city, he leapt and danced before the Lord with wild abandon. His wife, Michal, saw him and despised him, pained at the thought that others would see the king acting like a commoner. "How the king of Israel distinguished himself today!" she rebuked him. "He uncovered himself today in the eyes of his servants' maids as one of the foolish ones shamelessly uncovers himself!"

David responded to her, "It was before the LORD, who chose me above your father and above all his house, to appoint me ruler over the people of the LORD, over Israel; therefore I will celebrate before the LORD. I will be more lightly esteemed than this and will be humble in my own eyes..."[64]

In essence, he told her, "I do have gifts, and they are an expression of God working through me. He chose me, yes, but I am also a weak vessel. I am not ashamed to humble myself as creation before my Creator."

[64] 2 Samuel 6:16-23

113

We can describe exactly what a humble person looks like. Perhaps we think humility is marked by someone who doesn't drink alcohol, someone who wears certain clothes, someone who does certain jobs, or (in church) someone who washes others' feet at the right time. These sorts of markers have to do with the culture we come from, not with the spiritual discernment of humility. Humility is not an appearance and will look different depending on the gift of the person walking in it. Just as pride can be found in any action, so can humility. Humility is ultimately a heart attitude, birthed in the heart of love.

C. S. Lewis challenged his generation's picture of a humble person when he wrote,

> Do not imagine that if you meet a really humble man he will be what most people call "humble" nowadays: he will not be a sort of greasy, smarmy person, who is always telling you that, of course, he is nobody. Probably all you will think about him is that he seemed a cheerful, intelligent chap who took a real interest in what you said to him. If you do dislike him it will be because you feel a little envious of anyone who seems to enjoy life so easily. He will not be thinking about humility: he will not be thinking about himself at all.[65]

---

[65] C. S. Lewis, *Mere Christianity*.

Booker T. Washington, an educator, author, orator, and presidential advisor, was out walking shortly after accepting the presidency of the Tuskegee Institute in Alabama. As he passed through a wealthy part of town, a woman stopped him. Not recognizing the famous Professor Washington, she offered to pay him a small sum to chop wood for her. Professor Washington smiled, left his walk, and went about doing the humble chore she had requested. He split the logs, carried them inside, and stacked the wood near the hearth.

A neighbor girl recognized him and later told the lady who the man was who had chopped her firewood. Chagrined, the woman went the next day to see Professor Washington in his office at the Institute to apologize. "It's perfectly all right, Madam," he replied. "Occasionally I enjoy a little manual labor. Besides, it's always a delight to do something for a friend."

His act of humility won her loyalty, and she soon persuaded wealthy friends to join her in donating thousands of dollars to the Tuskegee Institute.[66]

---

[66] Story paraphrased from *Our Daily Bread.*

CHAPTER SEVEN

JESUS: PERFECT EXPRESSION OF A HUMBLE GOD

If humility is so foreign and pride so familiar, maybe it's because that is just the way we are, and we shouldn't worry about it. Join the dog-eat-dog world, fight for what you can get, and cut off anyone who won't help you get what you want. For a part of me, this makes sense. Another part of me remains unsatisfied, asking, "Is this all there is?" It seems like there should be more.

If humanity were our only standard, then we would all be fairly safe. Because we set the bar so low, most of us measure up as "good enough." However, there is a Light in our darkness—there is a Word in our conversations—there is a Spirit at work in our hearts. A standard exists that is higher than our own. Simply put, God has an answer to our darkened, meaningless, and rebellious lives.

God did not leave us alone to discover His beauty and terrifying humility by speculating about the life of heaven. To understand His humility in heaven will take an eternity—thankfully something He offers us—but it must begin in a more familiar place: here on earth. And that we can discover by looking to Jesus, the exact representation of God.[67] When the disciples asked Jesus for a sneak peek at the Father, the ultimate view, Jesus responded that if they had seen Him, then they had seen the Father.[68] So although we can't peek through the finite into the eternal, Jesus has revealed the eternal to us through the finite, and in His revelation, we see the humility of God.

God has more for us than fighting for life in a dog-eat-dog world. He made us in His image. He is not content to let us wallow in excrement when He has a feast in His heart to give to us. His answer is not an abstract, distant, but possibly relevant comment from His safety in heaven. He answered our struggle personally. Jesus is God's personal answer to our struggle with pride: the humility of God on display for all to see. He is the living model to show us the life for which God made us. He came to dwell among us to show us what he has always had in His heart for us, and what we must pursue if we want abundant life—*His* life—for there is no life outside of Him.

Jesus and Humility as Creation

When Jesus consented to become a human being, He willingly took our weaknesses and limitations upon

---

[67] Hebrews 1
[68] John 14:6

Himself. Philippians tells us that Jesus emptied Himself and took the form of a servant. When Jesus came to earth as a man, He essentially became weak to the extent that a virus could have taken Him out if God didn't watch over Him. He had limited energy, growing tired and needing rest; He had limits of spiritual resources, needing to go out daily in the mornings to be filled afresh from time spent with His Father. His insight was limited, so that he made mistakes (as distinguished from sin), such as when He thought at twelve years of age that it was time for Him to go to the temple in Jerusalem and start God's work there, when in fact He was not to begin His ministry until He was thirty.

All of this, however, is a more obvious and thus more written-about aspect of His character, and so let me approach the topic from a different perspective.

Being limited, we must be open to facing the pain that comes from vulnerability. If Jesus had any denial or fear of pain—if He lacked humility through not embracing weakness in Himself—He would not have been able to face it in others. We would have seen Him flinching, pulling away, or at least avoiding pain when He saw it. But when we look at His life, we find Him drawn to it:

- Jesus sees a man with a withered hand and calls him out in front of all the people in the synagogue.
- A woman caught in adultery is thrown at His

feet for judgment. The religious leaders stand there to accuse her, but He stays there and engages them all.

- He sees a grieving widow whose son has died. He feels her pain and has compassion. He raises her son from the dead.

- His friend Lazarus dies, and He weeps at his graveside.

- A man with a legion of demons comes running up to Him from the cemetery where he lives. Jesus engages him in a conversation, casts all the demons out, and then tells the man to share with his home town how God had mercy on him.

- While dining with religious leaders, He makes space for an immoral woman, who washes His feet with her tears, dries them with her hair, and anoints them with expensive perfume. Then He honors her before the whole company.

- He speaks honestly and vulnerably with a Samaritan woman, despite her questionable past, and despite the cultural wall between them (that no one wants Him to break through).

- On the sea in a storm, His disciples think death is only a wave away, and Jesus calms the storm and challenges them to have faith.

- A sick woman touches His garment in a crowded street, and He stops to find her. He acknowledges her pain and faith, and He encourages her.

There is no human condition of weakness that surprises Him or makes Him feel uncomfortable, from sickness to fear to sorrow to sin (which includes the pain of repentance). Why? Because He is humble. He knows all about us and is not surprised by anything. He is willing to face any human pain in the people He loves. He accepts His humanity and embraces it. He faces the pains and struggles with which we are all confronted and owns them.

Jesus and Humility as a Sinner

Unlike us, who sin and must face painful repentance and correction, Jesus responded to His Father first and did not sin. His life displays the opposite of each aspect of sinful pride as it is seen in us: the lust for power; competition; the attempt to appear unbroken; the fear of man; willful blindness and refusal of the truth; problems with authority; self-exultation; and caring about *appearing* rather than *being* (focusing on the outside).

He did not lust for power. This is the taproot, the very essence of the struggle for us. All other aspects of pride draw from this root within us. How does God view power? Even though He has all of it, He clearly does not obsess over it as we do, for He gave it all up. Jesus emptied Himself and laid His power aside. Inconceivable to us, perhaps, but it was a choice to express humility for Him. He went even farther, taking on the form of a servant. Servants, by definition, have no power and instead work to meet the needs of others, to help them grow. Jesus modeled to us that power is not the goal. Love in humility is.

Then Jesus took the ultimate step and gave up His life for us. It is almost as though the lust for power became so strong in us that the only way to wake us up and show us true humility was to become totally powerless, for us to see what was in His heart. If He retained the smallest regard for power, then He would never under any circumstances have chosen this route as the way to reveal Himself to us. Jesus was the perfect expression of God's humility.

He was not competitive. Competition says we have something to prove, something to justify. We want people to know we should be respected because of what we do. Not Jesus. He came to reveal His Father to us. He had a single audience, and His Father's pleasure was His primary desire. The simple truth is that He purposely chose to "lose" on a cross that so we might win the Father. He had nothing to prove but everything to reveal to those who wanted to see.

He did not strive to appear unbroken. He was the only human being to walk the earth since Adam and Eve who was not broken by sin, and yet He didn't clothe himself with arrogance. Instead, He took on our brokenness so that we wouldn't have to be broken anymore. This was a choice He made even though the thought of it was enough to make Him sweat blood. When He was dying on the cross and became broken for us, He wasn't ashamed of it and didn't try to hide it. He publicly cried out to His Father. At His lowest and most broken point, He expressed Himself for us to see.

He didn't live in the fear of man. Isaiah 11:3 says that He delighted in the fear of God; Isaiah 33:6 says it was His treasure. He didn't buy into our "marketing" but knew exactly what we were and had the capacity to do. This does not mean He didn't love or respect us; it means simply that He knew men could not define him. Therefore, He didn't pander to us or try to get us to like Him. John 2:24 says that Jesus knew what was in man, and He didn't entrust Himself to us. He had no illusions or popular optimism about us. The full story of humanity was crystal clear to Him.

He chose the truth and refused blindness. To be radical is to get to the core or root meaning of something. When you look at Jesus' life, that was how He lived: not by the letter of the law, but by its spirit. He always went for the very heart of God revealed in the law. He would take each situation and deal with the heart issues involved, even if it meant onlookers would not follow Him, as when the rich man walked away, reckoning the cost too high.[69] Jesus let him go. He dealt most harshly with those in religious authority, seeing their choice to hide in religion as evil. His death on a

---

[69] Matthew 19

cross was to be the defining point of truth in the Kingdom of God. It meant the truth of God must be honored
and followed, even if it cost you your life, and your
death was based on the deception of humanity.

He was always submitted to God's authority. He
was under God's authority in everything He did, even
through its expressions in the governmental institu-
tions of His day (Pilate), and even to the point of His
own death. His own authority in teaching was so clear
that people wondered at Him, asking, "Where did He
get such authority?" The secret was in His submission
to God's authority, for true authority can only come
from God. He even submitted to Pilate's authority to
accomplish the will of God.

He was not focused on self-exaltation. He knew His
value and place. He knew where He came from and
where He was going. Jesus came, the only one who
could truly exalt Himself, and it seems His greatest joy
outside of exalting His Father was to exalt us. He didn't
treat us like nothing but rather as having great value before God. He treated us as people chosen by God who
were lost but could be redeemed. The choice to humble
ourselves and accept this gift was ours to take or reject.
He had no illusions as to who we were, but He also was
very clear on what we could be in God's grace for us.

He was not focused on the outside. Over and over,
He would deal with the heart of people. He was most

angry at those who hid behind religion and only looked at the outside, calling them "whitewashed tombs,"[70] beautiful on the outside but inside full of hypocrisy and lawlessness. He knew that the inside was the right starting place for the Kingdom of God, and in time, cleanness within would lead to cleanness without.

Jesus and Humility as a Saint

Frankly, this is the hardest aspect of humility for me to define in reference to Jesus. Not because of His limitations, but because of *my* limitations and who He was. He was not a saint. He was the essence of all saints and so much more: God in human form. We have no comparison possible in this case. Each one of us expresses a small piece of God in the gift He has given of Himself to us; Jesus, however, was not *an* expression, He was *the* Expression, in its fullest and most profound sense. How can I add anything to this? I can't, but I must try. So with this in mind, let me attempt to look at this for what it might mean to us.

The essence of being a saint is not to do something but to *be* something. When we think of saints, we often think of a very religious person. (Almost without exception, we picture them wearing robes!) Perhaps they are monks or nuns who care nothing for the material things of this world. Shallowly, many might see Jesus

[70] Matthew 23:27

this way. But to do so would be limiting and short-sighted. He was not a priest—in fact, He worked in a down-to-earth profession, as a carpenter. So, if I lay our cultural assumptions about "sainthood" aside for a moment and reflect on Jesus' life, I begin to see a better picture of what He is like.

He calls twelve people to live and *be* with Him, and He has countless other disciples besides. He interacts with others, goes to parties, and even supplies some of the wine. He attends funerals and weeps. He eats meals with key leaders. He engages everyone He meets in a very personal way, connecting with them right where they are. He grows angry at religious leaders who hide behind the law when they should be the clearest expression of God, and He shows His anger by reprimanding them openly. He rebukes His disciples when they try to stop children from coming to Him, and He takes the children in His arms and holds them.

He does unbelievable miracles, but He does so without fanfare, knowing the performance of miracles does not give Him anything He does not already have. For instance, Jesus was walking on the water alone, noticed His disciples in a boat, and was going to pass them by. When they saw Him and called to Him, He joined them. He didn't care about being impressive. He didn't need the validation or marketing to prove anything. (From my very limited perspective in the world I live in, that alone qualifies Him as a saint!) He was fully, joyfully, and painfully human and still the essence of God.

Yet even so, we can learn from Him at every turn. Most especially, we can learn from how Jesus was never satisfied with anything less than His Father in the moment. He was fully present with God in each moment of the day. That was His joy, His life. Once, trying to retreat to rest with His disciples, the people find Him out.[71] Instead of sending them away, He teaches them and feeds them. He seems to have changed His plans because He saw their hunger, both spiritual and physical.

When I step back from my old mindset (i.e., "People who are really spiritual do religious work"), I start to find that it is possible to walk in humility as a saint in each of the domains of life. Business, Education, Arts, Government, Communication, Family, Science: whatever it be, the more people walk in their gifts, the more unique they become. What holds them together as an expression of God is the values that they live by.

In Jesus' life, and inevitably therefore in the lives of His saints, we find many common values:

Human life is sacred. Each person, made in the image of God, has value regardless of their choices. No matter how broken or arrogant, they must be treated with honor, dignity, and respect. Jesus never puts anyone in a box or accepts the cultural biases about them; instead, He engages each person as the people they are and were meant to be in God.

---

[71] Matthew 14

The material world is real and essential for life. When God created the material world, He said that it was good. We can see His goodness in that He created the material world for us that allows us to live and move and have our being. There is no division of the world into secular and sacred. It is all sacred to God.

Words have power, and we are responsible for them. God put His unfinished breath in us and gave us the creative ability to finish creation by naming aspects of it as Adam did with the animals. The words we choose are an expression of our heart and define how we relate to others. Jesus was the Word of God made manifest: its living, breathing expression.

Anything that takes us away from God's thinking destroys us (idolatry). The words we choose form ideas; ideas embraced grow into beliefs. And beliefs define the mental model we have, or the lines on which we frame life. Jesus lived the perfect expression of God in revealing God to us. As we grow, therefore, we seek to develop the mind of Christ as He revealed it.

Everything is redeemable. Since all of life is sacred and everything God made is good, we can redeem the world around us. Will we completely remove the fruit of the Fall? No, but we have made the mess, and a part of our responsibility is to work to clean it up.

The more light shines into places where darkness dwells, the more unique the dwellers therein become.

What makes people lose their unique expression of God is their lack of humility. The more fully they develop and express their gifts, the more unique they will become.

All good things come from God. Therefore, any good gift expressed, enjoyed, celebrated, and used to build value and life in families, communities, or nations, is an expression of God. That in its simplest essence is being and growing as a saint.

...

If there was any arrogance in God, any clinging to power, insecurity, ignorance, or pride, we can know this for sure: Jesus would not have come to live and dwell among us and then die a hideous death on a cross as a means to forgive us. Remember, that wasn't His own good idea; it was the will of His Father to represent Him in a way that was the purest expression of Himself. We are the ones who have polluted the well of humanity's life. We are the ones who have destroyed each other and this world. We are the ones who are killing ourselves with our arrogance.

Many years ago, I went skiing with my young son Joshua. We came to the rope tow and found ourselves in the company of many parents helping their young children to learn to ski. Some children rode between their mothers' or fathers' legs and skied down the hill.

Standing with Joshua, I looked back on the line and noticed a little boy, perhaps four years old, trying to get control of his skis. He began to run towards the line of people waiting, but soon he was moving faster than he could control. His mother, an experienced skier who had trained him right, yelled out, "Sit down!"

The boy sat down immediately. It worked like a wonderful brake, and he stopped short of the people without causing any damage. His mom helped him up—crisis averted—all was well.

When weak, or when we discover sin in our life, or when we sense God's Spirit stirring us to action, we need to hear our Father who yells out to us, "Humble yourself!" We must yield, bending the knee at once when we hear His voice calling us to humility, for it is our only hope. Then and then alone will the glory of God be manifest in our midst and the grace of God flow among us.

EPILOGUE

I Choose Humility

You and I face a choice. The stage has been set. Others have gone before us to prepare the way. The director has pointed to us. Our turn has come to enter the stage and play our part. What will you do?

With my limitations

When I am expected to know all things,
or when I know nothing…
> When others impose on me the status of a god,
> or ignore me and pretend I don't exist…
> When I am placed on a pillar as one who can
do no wrong,
> > or placed in humanity's trash bin
> > because I don't produce what they
> > demand…
> When I am faced with limitations
> and confronted with my own lack…

> I will embrace my weakness.
> ***I choose humility.***

With my sin

When I harden my heart to protect myself,
or when others break my heart and I am consumed
with hatred and refuse to forgive...
When I assert that the good I do outweighs the bad,
or when I refuse to admit or name the wrong I've
done...
When I hurt others and search for power so that I can
be in control,
or when others dominate me and I grow envious...
When I compete to win at any cost,
or when I despair of being better than anyone else...
When I care more for what people will say than what
God says...

I will repent.
I choose humility.

With my gifts

When I compare myself with others,
or feel insecure...
When I can't find the gift within me,
or when I think my gift is the most important gift...
When I use it only to get the praise of others,
or when I wither because I think my gift too small to
earn me attention or value...
Whether seen or unseen, great or small...
I will express my voice to my audience of One.

I choose humility.

No choice is too small. No pride is worth embracing. To know that by a simple act of my will I can please the Almighty, what blessedness is mine! It is enough to know His pleasure: the radiance of His smile as He dances over me with Joy.

Each time I make one simple, humble choice, I honor Him and model Him to an arrogant world.

How do we do it? With a simple starting place: letting Him in.

The starting place is the hardest place. The old saying goes, the journey of a thousand miles begins with a step. So the journey of humility begins with a step. Once again, C. S. Lewis puts words to the task before us:

> That is why the real problem of the Christian life comes where people do not usually look for it. It comes the very moment you wake up each morning. All your wishes and hopes for the day rush at you like wild animals. And the first job each morning consists simply in shoving them all back; in listening to that other voice, taking that other point of view, letting that other larger, stronger, quieter life come flowing in. And so on, all day.

Standing back from all your natural fussing and frettings; coming in out of the wind.[72]

While living in Hawaii, I loved to go for a bike ride in the afternoons. On one day, I got my bike out, strapped my helmet on, and started peddling. I was doing a ten mile ride, and the weather was beautiful. I seemed to be flying down the road, much faster than usual. I didn't feel the wind pushing me, nor see the effects of it on the trees or bushes I passed. *I'm in great form today,* I thought, pleased. *I must be in better shape than I thought.*

I made it out past the airport and then turned to come back. I was shocked to realize there was a strong wind pushing me the whole time. Now, the stiff wind buffeted me, shoving me back. I was shocked. It was time to ride into the wind, and suddenly the bike ride was a very different story. It now seemed like I needed to peddle just to go downhill. At that moment, I knew I needed to make a clear choice to push forward, complete the task ahead of me, finishing the "race" that I had set before me. I had enjoyed being pushed along, but now the real work began.

I am often reminded of that day when I have "turned" into a situation and am confronted with my own struggles of life. I have been enjoying it when things go well and life seems to push me forward; but then I need to change directions or do something different, and I real-

[72] C. S. Lewis, *Mere Christianity.*

ize I have my real work cut out for me. Time to "grow up." I have choices to make, and I had best buckle down and get serious. In those moments, the real work of life begins. I must humble myself, let life expose me, embrace it, bring God into it, and press on.

When you are confronted with the winds of life and you have turned into a challenge—when it seems like the "world" is against you—it is time to begin the real discipline of life. It is time to humble ourselves, to remind ourselves that our goal is to be like Christ, and to embrace what life exposes in us. I wish I could say it all gets easier as you get older. It doesn't. It is still a choice I must make on a daily basis. Yes, I am much more aware of the struggle, and I have seen victories in the past that encourage me, but I must reach out and choose to walk into those mercies that are new each morning.

Pray with me: Jesus, I need You. I can't do this on my own. I confess, I don't even know where to begin. But You are the God of new beginnings who can take ashes and bring new life. You conquered death and overcame my greatest fears. I take my broken heart and put it in Your hands. I trust You to teach me how to do this so that Your grace would be abundant in my life. Please, for Uour glory, give me humility that I might know Your grace and find abundant life.

Amen.

Humility

ABOUT THE AUTHOR

Matt Rawlins is CEO of Green Bench Consulting. He travels internationally as a trainer and consultant, dealing with leadership and organizational issues.

With a PhD in Communication, Matt has a heart to see people understand who they are and specifically, to help leaders communicate about difficult issues in times of change.

The author of 14 books, Matt is a gifted writer and communicator.

Matt currently resides with his wife Celia in Singapore.

You can contact him at: mrawlins@mac.com.

His business web site is: thegreenbench.com.